The Hot Mess Express

The Peterson Girls Adventures

Steffanie M. Peterson

35th Star Publishing
Charleston, West Virginia
www.35thstar.com

The Hot Mess Express

The Peterson Girls Adventures

#thepetersongirlsadventures
www.thepetersongirlsadventures.com

BIOGRAPHY & AUTOBIOGRAPHY / Personal Memoirs
PERFORMING ARTS / General
RELIGION / Christian Living / Inspirational
RELIGION / Christian Living / Personal Memoirs

ISBN-13: 978-0-9965764-9-9
ISBN-10: 0-9965764-9-5

35th Star Publishing - Charleston, West Virginia
www.35thstar.com

Cover design by: Studio 6 Sense – www. studio6sense.com

Dedication

To my dearest Hannah Jane.

Your dreams have taken us on an unimaginable journey over the last five and a half years. In fact, it's your dreams that made this book a reality. I remain in awe that God continuously gave me whatever I needed, in each situation or circumstance, to help you chase your dreams. Even more miraculous, is the way in which He used your dreams to ignite mine.

You inspire me every single day to be bolder in my faith and to love people deeper and without boundaries. You have taught me to work harder tomorrow than I did today. And to remember that a wonderful life is made up of a million tiny moments, not just one or two big ones.

Between the covers of this book are snapshots of a life (our life!) that was only possible because you trusted me to lead our little family into places far away and unknown. We still have mountains to climb, rivers to cross and valleys to journey through - but I know, beyond a shadow of a doubt, we will overcome any obstacle that comes our way as long as we are together.

Just promise me this - NEVER STOP DREAMING #babybird!

I love you more than the sun and the moon and the stars in the sky, Hannah Jane Peterson.

Contents

Acknowledgments

First, to my beloved Hannah Jane Peterson. Without you, there would be no reason for this adventure. You are the reason I get out of bed every day. You are the reason my heart continues to beat. Keep dreaming #babybird. The world is yours.

To Hannah Jane's teachers and mentors: Kristy Cates, Lauren 'Coco' Cohn, KT Sullivan, Jon Weber, Jon Nelson, Jeff Statitle, Arri Simon, Greg Parente and Marc Tuminelli. Thank you doesn't seem enough, but it's what we have to give at this moment in our journey. My deepest thanks for investing in her and believing in her (OUR!) dreams. You set the bar high and never allowed her to settle for "good enough." You pushed her into uncomfortable spaces that forced her to grow as a human and as a performer. She is who she is today, because you were the teachers/mentors you were when she needed it most.

To the best 'BFF' any girl could ask for, Susan Brasselle. Thank you for your unwavering love, support and friendship. You ARE the wind beneath my wings.

To the one who never tires of hearing us talk about our dreams. My daddy and #babybird's Grandpoppy, James 'Jim' Myers. You have always been our biggest cheerleader, ready to hear about even the smallest details of this journey. We could never have done this without you!

To the master show photographer and videographer, David Rosen. You captured things I couldn't and you shared your work so graciously. You truly are a wonderful human and I am so unbelievably thankful that you have documented the most precious moments of this journey so far. We will cherish every one of them for the rest of our lives.

To the best boss anyone could ask for, Dr. Matthew White. You gave me the freedom to be a mom when she needed me most. I am forever grateful for the love and support you and Cindy have shown both of us the last few years.

To the uncountable family and friends who have supported us from day one. Your phone calls, texts, emails, social media posts, visits and care packages gave us the encouragement we needed to keep pushing forward toward our dreams.

To the man who made my dreams of writing a book a reality. My friend-turned-family-turned-publisher, Steve Cunningham. You made this book possible and I will forever be grateful for your (and Laura's!!) selfless support of BOTH our dreams.

To my God.
My Lord and Savior.
Without You, there is nothing.

Edelweiss

A simple white flower from the daisy family, Edelweiss is truly a botanical wonder. Found primarily in the high altitudes of the Swiss Alps, this beautiful plant thrives in the harshest climate conditions. Often found with two flowers per stem, Edelweiss blooms in a star-like formation.

When most people hear the word Edelweiss, they immediately think of the song from *The Sound of Music*. What they don't realize is that there is a romantic story behind the beautiful flower.

History reveals to us that bringing a bouquet of Edelweiss was considered to be the ultimate expression of a man's love. Because of the location of these flowers, many men lost their lives trying to gather them from the steep mountains and icy ledges where they grew. Those that were successful, were considered courageous with serious intentions.

We moved to New York City with very serious intentions. We were fully committed the moment we stepped out of that rental truck. I now realize that moving to this big, cold city took more courage that I even realized we had.

I am thankful every day that I didn't put too much time into making the decision to move. Had I stopped long enough to actually think about what I was doing, I probably would not have had the courage to take the leap of faith that brought us on this adventure.

The good news is, somewhere between closing my apartment door for the last time in West Virginia and opening my apartment door for the first time here in NYC, we found our courage.

Like the Edelweiss, we stick together and have adapted to our new surroundings that have been challenging to say the least. In a city that can be cold and harsh, we continue to thrive, just like those delicate flowers growing against all odds in the Swiss Alps.

Write a Book, They Said

Write a what?

I have never written a book. If I am telling the truth, I never thought about writing one either. That is until people started saying "you have to write a book!" I remember thinking to myself, why would I do that? Would people really want to read the ridiculousness that has turned into #thepetersongirlsadventures? I still don't know the answer to that question, but somewhere along the way I felt a stir deep in my soul that I needed to write this book. So here we go.

When I sat down and started to make a list of what I might include, I was genuinely worried I would not have nearly enough material. Ironically, in the end I had so much to share I actually had to cut nearly as much as I included. I want you to know, I really tried to pull the best of the best to share with you!

My Mama always told me that words came to life under my hands. With the click of a few keys, I could make words dance across the page. For years my girlfriends always called me when they needed to send "the perfect message" to their latest flame to

1

scoot them off into the sunset. I always found it a weird predicament to be in, but secretly enjoyed it because the process of creating came so naturally to me.

I knew the moment our adventure began I needed to record the ups and downs of this journey so that Hannah Jane and I could revisit the good times when life got difficult. It was never intended for public viewing because, quite frankly, this journey is littered with some crazy stuff and a lot of it isn't particularly pretty. If I was going to go to these lengths to tell our story (I mean, writing a book isn't an easy task), I had to accept the fact that I had to be honest about the real challenges we faced because that is what makes our story so amazing. Packing up and moving to NYC with a starry eyed, barely a teenage daughter who wanted to go to Broadway is no joke. Don't get me wrong, we have had a total blast these last five years. At least most of the time. But it's also been hard. And when I say "hard" what I really mean is "sitting in the fetal position" hard some days.

Some parts of our story are pretty embarrassing. Some of them are just plain silly. And, some of them I still haven't figured out how they even made the cut to begin with. All I know is that somewhere in the process of pulling this together, my gut told me to leave them in, so I am going with the notion that these not so flattering instances are going to help someone dig deep and not feel so alone on their own journey.

If this book ultimately helps someone pick up their dream and run with it, I am happy to be the outspoken, unashamed, not so perfect, hot mess of an inspiration. Who am I kidding? I've pretty much been all of those things my whole life anyway, so I might as well embrace the nonsense and share it with everyone else!

Let's get one other thing straight. I NEVER planned to move to New York. I also never planned to be a divorcee with a young girl who had a passion for something bigger than I had ever dreamed for myself. I never imagined living without my own Mama. I never even considered the fact that this girl and I would climb mountains bigger than either of us could even see the top of.

By the time Hannah Jane was about ten years old, most of those things were true of our life. She had been bitten by the theater bug and was totally convinced that she would move to NYC after high school graduation. She was determined to get to Broadway and no one was going to stand in her way. Not even her overprotective Mama. She used to say, "Mama, it's my destiny to be on Broadway." I would just laugh and think to myself how she was going to change her mind one hundred times between now and then and ultimately end up being a veterinarian or a nurse. She loves animals and taking care of people, so I was fairly confident that was going to be her path. Boy, was I wrong. She knew exactly what she wanted, and to this day she remains 1000% committed to that dream.

As you will learn, this was all completely out of the blue. And it happened FAST. It was so unexpected. There was NEVER a plan to move her to NYC n- at least not at thirteen years old! The only real plan I had was to make sure she had food, shelter, and an education. My job was to raise her to be a kind, compassionate human who would make this world a better place. Anything beyond that was more than my little brain could process.

But here we are. The truth is I AM a single, forty-something mom. I have this amazing young woman who has been given this beautiful gift that she uses to touch people's hearts. My sweet Mama did leave this earth way too soon. And, we ARE climbing mountains that we still can't see the top of - every single day. Some days we fly up those mountains like they are little mole hills. Other days we barely make it two feet. And some days we don't move at all. I can tell you this much; not a day goes by that we don't set our eyes to what lies ahead. We may not always feel like we have the strength to push forward, but we are always looking at the future knowing we will get there, one step at a time.

Our life's path has not been a yellow brick road that would lead us to the all-knowing Wizard who would whisk us away to the perfect little place where life is easy and predictable. We have not glided through each day as if we were on a fresh slab of ice just waiting for life's etchings to be painted across it with every perfect stride of our ice skates. In fact, our journey has been quite the opposite. Our journey more closely resembles a hiking path littered with rocks, holes and gaps so large we thought we might fall to our death a time or twenty. But we didn't. Sure, we tripped and stumbled a lot, trust me. But we are still standing! We are making strides towards that dream every single day.

We have encountered so much grace. The kind of grace that only comes from a loving God. (Seriously, people, wait until I talk finances later on. You will laugh at first, but then you will scratch your head in complete wonder of how in the world we survived that first year. You really will.) It was God's grace that stretched my finances. It was God's grace that found us a place to live. It was God's grace that connected us time and time again to amazingly talented performers and industry executives. It was God's unfailing grace that kept my fingers moving and the words flowing to even tell you our story.

I feel like I need to preface what you are about to read. This is not a perfect book. It's my first go at this, and while I love writing, I am human and make mistakes. Often. When you spot a typo or a run-on sentence, just giggle to yourself and try to imagine in which crazy place I was writing that particular section.

I won't exhaust the list here, but I can tell you that 90% of this book was written somewhere other than on my computer. I wrote while commuting on the subway, walking down the street, sitting on my couch, waiting on shows to start or during intermission, propped up in my bed with three cats on my lap, in the gynecologist waiting room, on an airplane, the bus and at least a dozen more places that for one reason or another you probably don't need to hear.

Yes, before you say out loud to yourself, "did she not proofread it?" Of course, I did! What I didn't do was send it to a big fancy editor in some high rise building in Manhattan to critique. I feared that someone on the outside might try to change it in some way that would steal the integrity of my vision. I wanted you to read this as if we were having a conversation. Relaxed, and with humor. Which means, the grammar isn't perfect. Collective gasp, I know. But I don't really care about the grammar or punctuation or minor spelling errors.

I care about the story.

Just like everything else in my life, I wanted to see this through. I said that I would do it and I was determined to do just that. Start to finish. Once I got started, I quickly realized there was no way I could do this alone. So I called on my tribe!

I had people read sections and tell me if they made any sense at all. I had a book reading party to give me some encouragement that people might actually want to read this hot mess of a story. If you were held captive by me on one of my "can I just read you this chapter?" days – bless you.

But, there is no way this would have been a reality without my pal, Steve Cunningham, of 35th Star Publishing. The Cunningham family is part of our roots. They go deep into our history. Steve has a small publishing company and when I told him I was writing a book, he immediately offered his help. If I could write it – he could publish it! I thank God every day he did because I would have never been able to do this on my own in any reasonable amount of time. As you'll read throughout our story, God has impeccable timing and always shows up just when we need it most. The Cunningham family is just one example of His perfect timing.

This is MY story. The story that unfolded before my eyes. Hannah Jane has a different story. Yes, they are very similar, but she had her own set of emotions and challenges that stretched into places that I just couldn't go because I wasn't the one on stage or at endless auditions. She was. And from where I sat, she navigated it beautifully. Not to say there weren't any bumps and many Mom talks along the way, because there were - LOTS! And with each one our mother-daughter relationship grew a little closer. Which makes our story even more special. It wasn't just about the journey. It was about the relationship that blossomed between us in the process. A relationship that would have never happened had we been a normal family with a mom, a dad, a perfect little house, in a perfect little neighborhood. We embraced our little family and dove into whatever adventures came our way!

If this book, with all of its imperfections, inspires just one single person to chase a dream that they have buried in their hearts because they didn't think they could do it - then every moment, every tear, every mistake, every challenge, and every raw emotion was worth it. 1000%. I hope you laugh. I hope you scratch your head in wonder. I hope you cry a little. But what I really hope is that someone will pick up this book and be encouraged to take their own leap of faith. That someone finds the courage to jump into whatever it is they keep thinking about, but are too afraid to reach for. I want someone to put this book down and say to themselves, "if those darn Peterson girls did it, so can I."

Now, sit back, relax and enjoy the craziness that is *The Hot Mess Express: The Peterson Girls Adventures*.

-Steffanie

#thepetersongirlsadventures

CHAPTER ONE

The Egg, the Sperm, and the Embryo

Let's start at the very beginning.

Details are important, but I guess saying she started as "an egg" is probably a little too obvious. That is also probably a bit too much information! For those of you that know us well, feel free to skip this chapter. Everyone else, read on. Because you have to know who Hannah Jane was as a kid to embrace the nonsense that is our journey!

Hannah Jane Peterson was born on a very, VERY cold January day in Chicago, Illinois. She was about 7 hours shy of her due date, which should have been a clue about how her life would unfold. She was a little on the small size with 10 tiny fingers and 10 tiny toes, big blue eyes, and a sweet button nose. Those eyes, though. They were big. Think crazy alien, half of her face big. Blue as could be - but still big. She didn't cry when she came out, so her first spanking was almost immediate. Luckily for her (and me) there hasn't been a need for many of those since then—except for that incident with the remote control and the key pad imprint on the back of her leg when she was about a year old. Oh, but who needs details like that. I mean, it was like 18 years ago. Next time you see her, just ask her. It's a story she likes to tell because it wasn't necessarily my finest parenting moment.

Somewhere along this journey since leaving West Virginia (WV), Hannah Jane and I began calling each other Mama Bird and Baby Bird. Neither one of us can remember exactly when it happened, but it just stuck. I'm not as cool as she is, but in my attempt to be 'relevant,' for the rest of this book she is going to be known as #babybird.

Just shy of two years old, #babybird's dad and I moved back to my hometown of Charleston, WV. My mom had been diagnosed with cancer and honestly, the city was wearing us out. Two parents working full time with a tiny baby, a couple cats and two dogs was way more than I think either of us were prepared to handle. Her dad and I divorced when she was very young and so for most of her life it's been just us girls and always a few cats! As she grew, we became increasingly more like sisters and friends rather than mother and daughter.

I have heard the "you need to be her mother, not her friend" nonsense for years. I firmly believe for some kids, that's 100% necessary. But for us, this worked. She always knew there was a line. It was fine and sometimes more like a shade of gray, but there was definitely a line. And she knew when she crossed it. Thankfully, I think I can count on only two hands how many times that has happened. As our relationship grew, people started to call us "The Peterson Girls." I don't think any of them truly realized how deep our love for *The Gilmore Girls* really went. In our minds this nickname made us feel even more like we were walking in the footsteps of Lorelei and Rory Gilmore. Except I don't date and the only boy #babybird has really had an interest in is a statue named 'Tony' - as in a Tony Award for you non-Broadway people. I am sure that will change for both of us as our story continues to be written, but for now, it's just how our life looks.

By the time she could walk, she was climbing on anything she could to perform. She was always "making a show" even before we had any clue she could sing. In pre-school it was a regular occurrence for me to find photos in her cubbie of her "latest performance" for the kids and teachers in her class. They all told me "someday she's going to make it big and we can say we knew her when..." Her desire to make people happy started all the way back then. She loved when people smiled. She didn't even care much that some of them were actually laughing at what they could only describe as just pure nonsense play. But she didn't care. She was determined to show the world her skills.

When she was about four, I began listening to mainstream music again. Up until then, our household had been filled with a mixture of children's music, the American Songbook and contemporary Christian. I just wanted to be sure that what I put into her head was positive. Her little brain was forming with every passing second and I took my job to bring her up to be a good human very seriously. But I also loved a good country diva. At the time, Carrie Underwood had just won American Idol and she dominated my car CD player. Yes, kids, eighteen years ago CD players were a thing. She would dance and sing along from the back seat kicking her legs and bouncing her head to the beat. Little did I know how much she was actually soaking in.

One rainy Saturday afternoon when she was about four, she marched into the kitchen and said "I want to sing a song for you, Mommy, please sit down now." Well, when she says sit - you sit.

I sat, as instructed, and without missing a beat the concert began. "Cause I dub my tee into the side of his pretty wittle souped up four-wheel dribe, carved my name into your leather seeeeeeeets. I took a louismille slubber to both headlights, slashed a cole in all four tires. Maybe next time he'll think before he cheats." Minus a few phonetic issues, my four-year-old just sang of heartbreak, cheating and revenge and I was speechless. Once I got past the subject matter, I was stunned. She was on pitch. She was confident. She was determined to hold my eyes for her whole song.

And that is where it started.

With a song about heartbreak, cheating and revenge.

Her career was off to a good (I mean rocky) start for sure. I am positive my mother of the year trophy began to tarnish that day.

A few months after her declaration in our kitchen, I was helping a sweet friend with his small garden wedding. The bride, the groom and I were in the house scouting alternative locations for the ceremony as it appeared it was going to rain. When we returned to the garden, our mouths dropped to the ground when we realized what had transpired in our absence. Somehow this not-quite-five-year-old had convinced all the remaining adults, about fifteen family members and a few close friends, to stand in a line and sing *Supercalifragalisticexbealidocious*. She was standing on a chair conducting her "choir" when we arrived on the scene. Later in the day we joked with one of the brothers and asked how that came about. He said "She told us to line up and sing, so we did. None of us were going to tell her no." Yes, it started that early, folks. And if you have a tiny budding performer in your house, I am certain you have a similar story to share.

Not long after the garden incident, she auditioned for the Appalachian Children's Chorus, the official children's chorus of the state of West Virginia. She began singing with them as she entered kindergarten. This is where we would meet the string of musicians that would teach and cultivate her love for music that would ultimately lead us to NYC. The beauty of these people is that none of us really knew what was to come. All they wanted to do was help this little girl, who had a little talent, to do something that she loved. In all honesty, I didn't put her in lessons because I thought she would be famous someday. I just knew she loved to sing and dance. My best friend in high school was an amazing singer and I learned so much from watching her journey. This might have been one of God's earliest interventions in getting me ready for this kid to come into my life – to send me a best friend that was a ridiculous musician, in every sense of the word, so I could learn through osmosis! It was Tiffani who first introduced me to the wonders of Broadway. Oddly enough, the first Broadway soundtrack I fell in love with just happens to be one of #babybird's dream roles - Eva Perone.

Of course, she loved every lesson, every week. She was enamored with Ms. Noel, her teacher. So much so, that she was always the last to leave. Over time the teacher/student relationship developed into so much more. We became friends. A single mom herself, Noel and I connected, each having only one child with impressive musical abilities. Her sweet son, Noah, has turned into an amazing drummer and even though he won't do it often, he has quite the set of chops, too! #babybird became her "peanut" and it seemed like our lives as friends paralleled the early days of her musical journey. And Noel wasn't just teaching her. She was teaching me, too. I was listening to Noel groom #babybird's voice, her spirit, and her curiosity for music. Luckily some of this came naturally to me. In my school years I played instruments in the marching and concert bands and was a majorette. I was even the featured twirler my senior year.

Fast forward a few years and #babybird has decided to audition for her first musical. Mind you, she has had lots of chances to "sing" in front of people. She has even begun to sing in other languages. You see, to study with Ms. Noel, students were always expected to sing more than just the fun stuff. They were challenged with foreign language pieces, arias, and choral duets and trios. But this was different. This was just for fun.

The musical was *Annie*. Honestly, we were just hoping to be cast as an orphan! Yes, a great little ensemble role to learn and see if this theater thing was even for us. I remember the audition day like it was yesterday. She was so little on that stage. She sang as beautiful as ever. *Tomorrow*. Because if you want to be in Annie, you sing *Tomorrow*. This was the only audition I have ever been able to watch. In the real world of theater, you wait outside in the appropriate waiting room for parents. Yep, that is the hardest part, mom and dad. But don't worry, there is a whole chapter on what your role is in all this. And I promise you have a VERY IMPORTANT part to play.

She did some improv. We had NO IDEA what improv was, so when the director said that I remember looking at her, thinking "Oh, my baby, I am so sorry I didn't prepare you for this. Please forgive me." Not only did the kid forgive me, but she blossomed right before my eyes. She pranced and played across that stage as if she had been doing improv scenes her entire life. I sat there simply stunned. I would love to tell you this is when it hit me that this life was before us, but it didn't. I was a blubbering parent fighting back tears as my little nine-year old owned that stage like it was her J-O-B.

To our complete shock she was cast as .... *Annie*. WHAT??? I even asked the director when he called to offer the part, "Are you sure you meant to call Hannah Jane Peterson?" He laughed and said "Yes, ma'am, I know who I called." Adam Bryan was the new director of the Alban Arts and Conference Center in St. Albans, West Virginia, and was putting on his first show there. He went straight for the crowd pleaser for sure.

Adam would be #babybird's first director and the one who put the fire in her belly for this business. Adam was great. He was fun, young, and energetic about kids and acting. He knew he was getting a newbie and he handled her with much care. He taught her what she needed to know in a way she could understand and apply. He lovingly reminded her many times that she wasn't allowed to say other people's lines just because they forgot them during rehearsal. He groomed her to be the *Annie* he imagined. And she flourished with every moment. She made it her mission to be ready for every rehearsal. She began her life mantra of "go the extra mile" at the tender age of nine and even today, carries that with her into every musical adventure she encounters.

Annie sold out, night after night after night. They even added an extra show to accommodate people still calling for tickets. We went all out. I helped with costuming and marketing. The kid was on every radio and TV show we could find - every community promo that would have us. Her run as *Annie* also marked the first of many times that she would sing the National Anthem at local events. We even dyed her hair red and set it on perm rods for every show so she wouldn't have to mess with a wig.

Hundreds of family and friends came to support her and we made sure to see every single one. Little girls came dressed as *Annie* and looked at her with wide eyes as if she WAS the real *Annie*. Strangers stopped us and gushed with gratitude for transporting them back to a simpler time where courage triumphed and love ultimately won.

That's when I knew.

Our life's course was about to change. She was at home on the stage. She looked the way I feel all snuggled in my 'comfies' on the couch on a Sunday afternoon. It was where she belonged. It was where her heart desired to be more than anywhere else.

And so, it began. She auditioned and was cast in many shows after that one. She was invited to sing at festivals, community and sporting events and musical competitions. We learned A LOT in the early days. I became especially savvy at the technology side of things. Tracks, CD's, mics and all that stuff. I was also the sheet music getter and the costume manager. And, just like every other parent, I was also the chef, the chauffeur, the laundromat, the banker, and just plain old mom.

Through it all, she continued to grow in her craft, and I continued to learn new ways to help her and keep her focused on school at the same time. Sixth and seventh grades were so much fun for her. She finally got the chance to work every day with her second musical mentor, Mr. Brian Vannoy. He was her choir director with the Appalachian Children's Chorus, as well as her elementary school and middle school music teacher/choir director. Mr. Brian (as we affectionately called him) always looked for new ways to challenge #babybird. He wanted to see her love of music grow past just singing and into theory and performing.

Her last hometown show was exactly nine days before we pulled out for NYC. She closed our West Virginia chapter in a "big" way, playing Tracy Turnblad in *Hairspray, Jr.* It didn't occur to me until much later the irony of that character being her send off. Tracy was relentless. No matter what her story threw at her, she overcame. She was a bit naive, mixed with a little sass. Of all the adjectives I could pick, I would choose the exact same ones to describe the young woman #babybird has become over the last five years.

And that's how we came to the biggest crossroads of our lives. We had to make a choice. We could stay in our warm little town filled with friends and a life we truly loved. Or, we could take a giant leap of faith towards an adventure that we couldn't even begin to imagine.

We chose the adventure.

CHAPTER TWO

I Knew Better

But I did It anyway!

This book is essentially about our adventures AFTER we got to NYC. But you can't tell that part of our story without sharing how the stars aligned to send us off to NYC in the first place.

Everyone knows we moved, but most people don't know how things unfolded to get us to that pivotal point of actually taking the leap. Usually people say, "she moved to NYC so her daughter could chase her dreams of being on Broadway." A single mom, at 41, with a kid barely a teenager, was expected to think carefully about life decisions. And without the back story, it would be very easy for you to speculate that I made some stupid, rash decision without thoughtful preparation. After all, how many people do you know that would just pack it all up and move to a huge city on the wings of a dream?

None? Well, now you can say you know one. Me.

People assume that we just threw caution to the wind and took off on a willy-nilly adventure searching for fame. I have even had people say that I "sacrificed the safety and well-being of my daughter for something that would never work out." Yes, I know. People are mean. And I wish I could say that was the only mean thing that was ever said about us, but I can't. I had to make the decision pretty early on to not allow the negativity to take up residence in my mind. There was no room for nonsense. I had a million other thoughts that I could actually control and I wasn't about to let the negativity imposed by someone else take up even the tiniest space in my brain. I had bigger things to think about.

Anyone who would say something negative about us, and our journey, clearly doesn't know us, or our story.

Moving to NYC may have seemed like a quick decision to anyone on the outside looking in, but those people in our inner circle knew this had been brewing for years. I knew early on that she was born to be on a stage. I fully expected her to want to go into the entertainment business. I just didn't know if SHE would choose this life for herself. But I was 100% certain it was something she would wrestle with when it was time to start thinking about her career. Little did I know, she would have this all figured out before she celebrated her first double digit birthday.

This was never more evident than during the intermission of the opening night of *Annie*. She ran off the stage and said "Mama! Mama! I am going to do this for the rest of my life!" I guess if you want to get technical about this adventure, you could say that this all started nearly five years before we ever set foot in this city. Fast forward four years from that opening night and we found ourselves presented with an opportunity that neither one of us ever expected.

It was the winter of 2013. I will never forget that year. That's the year we lost my Mama. After a long, hard fought battle with multiple types of cancer, Nana met Jesus face to face and we were left with a hole in our hearts that only she could fill.

My Mama loved three things: rain, yellow roses and cake. I kid you not. It POURED on the day of her funeral. I mean "go get your twins and the Ark" kind of rain, not some little spring shower. Since that day, every single time #babybird has had a significant audition or performance, it rained at some point in the day. No lie. Every. Single. Time. And that is how I know she is always with us. I have a picture in my head of her sitting on a beautiful porch in heaven looking down on us with pride that only a Mama and Grandma can understand, her thousand-watt smile glowing all the way down to us, lighting our way.

On that cold Saturday, #babybird was starting to get sick. I had some errands to run, so I dropped her off at her grandpa's so she could rest and not be alone. She had two back to back performances that weekend, so she had to muster up enough energy to get through them. While I was out, I received a text from a friend that said "Did you know Disney is in town and that they are at the Marriott today? You should take her to audition."

Let me make something clear. I had known about these "auditions" for years. People coming in and out of small towns trying to find families that would "invest" their hard-earned money with these "professionals" who were going to make their kid a star. Once or twice a year they would come through Charleston, and I firmly (but kindly) said "no thank you" every time someone suggested we go. I knew what they were after and I didn't have it to give. We lived on a pretty tight budget (still do!), and the thought of essentially giving away my pennies to a stranger was something I just wasn't willing to do. I needed every single one of those pennies to take care of us.

Hear this loud and clear. I knew better.

I knew better.

I knew better.

Have you committed that to memory yet? Just in case you haven't, let me help you. I KNEW BETTER.

Here is where things go a little sideways in our story. Despite knowing better (in case you have forgotten, see above) on that cold Saturday morning something in my gut began pulling me in a different direction. For some crazy reason, I began to think that we needed to do this. I remember getting massive resistance from the kid. She was tired and sick, and she just didn't want to go. I backed off and let her rest a bit, but I just couldn't shake the thought that we were supposed to be there. Rarely in our lives have I ever had to pull the "mom card," but that day I did. I dragged her off the couch, and with grandpa in tow, off we went with no clue how much that one day would change our lives forever.

When we arrived, the first thing I did was scan the room just to take in the situation. To my surprise, it looked like there were maybe 150-200 people plus family and friends who had tagged along to watch the fun. They stepped up one at a time to perform for what appeared to be two very nice ladies. When it was her turn, #babybird bounced right up and proceeded to belt *At Last* by Etta James. Interesting choice of songs for a twelve-year-old, I know. She had just sung this in a friend's wedding, so it was fresh on her mind. Since we didn't really prepare for this, she just pulled it out of her head as we drove down the street toward the Marriott.

As soon as she opened her mouth, the ladies behind the table began to smile. It always happened like this. People would take one look at this little girl and expect to hear one thing, but something else entirely came out of her mouth. The look of shock was real. One even took a video. (Don't forget, I knew better.) After she finished singing, they clapped and told her what a great job she did. She thanked them for their kind words, and we headed home. In the car Grandpa and I told her how proud we were of her and pretty much dropped it from there.

Later that evening it happened. The email that I had suspected would come showed up in my inbox. It was from Kim Myers of ARTS International, the organization that she had performed for earlier in the day. Now, if I were a person who believes in signs this would have been a big flashing one like the "Hot Now" Krispy Kreme ones. (Side note: To this day no matter what car I am driving, it always has to make a stop there. I have convinced myself it's in the mechanics of the car, but my random passengers have yet to think that is the case.) Myers is my maiden name. It's a rare occasion to find it spelled without the 'e' before the 'y.' It seemed irrelevant at the time, but looking back, I am pretty sure that was from the Big Man upstairs. It was His way of gently showing up in in the midst of my uncertainty.

She made it clear that she LOVED #babybird and wanted us to come to a call-back for her program. As flattered as we were, I was honest and told her I was all for helping #babybird achieve her dreams, but I was a single mom with limited financial resources. I also let her know that we were booked all weekend with shows and rehearsals and there was just no way to be in two places at once. I truly thought that would be the end of that.

But it wasn't.

We exchanged several emails over the course of the evening and with every exchange, my mind raced. I just couldn't shake the thought that this was different. I finally decided that the only way to put that doubt to bed was to meet with her. After all, it was just a conversation. I wasn't committing to anything. (Because, you guessed it. I KNEW BETTER!) For the remainder of the night my mind was like a hamster wheel, spinning around all the reasons why this was a bad idea.

Monday came and #babybird had gotten sicker. The plan was to meet Kim, stay for ten minutes, and then get her home and back to bed. One of my favorite sayings starts with "the best laid plans." My plan was to get in and get out. I just knew that all I needed was that ten minutes to put my mind at rest and move on with our lives.

Clearly God had other plans for us that day. From the moment I laid eyes on Kim Myers, I knew something was different and the closure that I needed wasn't going to come easy. Kim introduced us to her business associate, Linda, and then began to explain who she was and what ARTS was all about. Her company did not represent talent. She made that very clear from the start. Her company gave dream chasers an opportunity to be on a larger stage, in front of industry executives. These "industry executives" (and, let's be honest, I didn't even know what an industry executive was at this point) were from all walks of the entertainment business. There was everyone from casting directors to talent agents and managers, to college recruiters offering scholarship opportunities. She was inviting us to be part of her fully produced international talent showcase. That was it. No expectations that #babybird would be catapulted to stardom over a long weekend in Florida.

Even though I knew better, the longer we talked, the more I began to realize that my curiosity was going to get the better of me. I wasn't going to be able to just say "sorry, we aren't interested." I had to know more.

So I began to ask questions. Lots of questions.

She answered every one of them without fluff or hesitation. She made no crazy promises. She was simply offering an opportunity. She made no guarantees that we would leave Florida and Hannah Jane would be signed with a NYC agent. She said, "ARTS is a place where performers can test out their wings, take master classes and make connections." In other words, network, network, network. It was a soft (and safe) introduction to the big, often times harsh, world of entertainment.

I remember thinking, "Lady, we have already tested our wings and they work just fine, thank you." I already knew she would fly when the time was right - somewhere after she went to college and got a practical degree that could support her financially. That was the plan. We just needed to stick to the plan.

Kim finished her explanation and began to talk specifically about #babybird. She said, "I get a good feeling about you two." My first reaction was: Yes, TWO. We are a package deal and we will remain that way for a very long, long time. Don't get any funny ideas that you are going to pitch my starry-eyed kid and think I will just follow her little dream chasing heart all the way to Florida. Nope, not this Mama. (Remember - I KNEW BETTER!)

As our time came to an end, she said something I will never

forget. "I am not asking you to commit to a major life change, but wouldn't it be good to just let her perform, get some feedback from people working in this industry, and make some connections so when she is ready, she goes in with eyes wide open?" I couldn't argue with that. Not one word of that was shady or even questionable. At that moment, everything within me wanted to say "no, thank you" and run before I got sucked into something bigger than I could handle.

She didn't push. She left it at that, said goodbye and said she would give us some time to mull it over and be in touch. I looked into #babybird's eyes as we walked away and instantly knew that she was feeling exactly the same way I was. *Have we met someone that isn't what we are supposed to watch out for? She seems like a normal person, but are we missing something?* I mean sometimes a serial killer looks normal, but that doesn't mean they still aren't a serial killer.

At this point, I realized I needed to at least do some more research before I put this to bed once and for all. Otherwise my poor mind would always wonder what might have happened if I had only given it some honest to goodness thought. Once I did some research, I was sure that I was going to find all kinds of reviews about ARTS being a scam, and that this seemingly nice lady was really a money-monger who just traveled around the world swindling people like Harold Hill from *The Music Man*. I was still living the battle in my brain between the "what if?" and the "I know better." But the more we talked, the scales had shifted slightly and the "I know better" was quickly losing ground to the "what if?" The only real way to calm down this madness in my head was to prove my "I know better" theory correct.

If you know me at all, you know that once I pick up the scent of something, I don't let it go easily. It's that never give up attitude that tends to get me in trouble. But it's also the same attitude that has kept us afloat the last five years, so it can't be all bad. For the next three days I spent every spare moment researching her and her company. I must have read a hundred reviews and not one single review had anything bad to say about this woman. NOT ONE. I figured I had to just be missing the bad ones, so I continued to dig. Nothing. I found absolutely NOTHING to discredit her or our conversation. In fact, I found nothing but positive. I even found well known performers who went through her program and said it was such a great step in their career. Because three nights of research is never enough, I spent every free moment I had the rest of that week digging. I found out her husband's name and Googled the heck out of him, too. But still, no dirt.

The following week, she reached out via email to "check in." Before I realized it, I had responded that we were interested. WHAT? Wait a minute. I KNEW BETTER. What was I doing? I didn't completely know how much this whole endeavor was going to cost. Could I even afford it? Could I get time off work to take her? But no matter how many obstacles my mind threw up, my gut said the same thing over and over. Something feels right. Just take the chance already.

Of course, no one in my life was going to be on board with this. We already struggled with paying for lessons and a myriad of other things that seemed to be pulling her in the direction of this career. Plus, I had been the LOUDEST one saying "don't get sucked in!" How in the world was I going to explain my sudden change of heart? The worry that people would see me as an irresponsible single mom was trying its best to take over space in my brain. But my gut was determined to convince my head that we needed to take this step out in faith. I just knew in my heart something special awaited us on the other side.

For most of our time as a duo, I felt like I was always explaining or justifying my parenting. None of my friends were divorced, so I always felt like I didn't measure up to the 'good parent' scale. If we got sucked into some scam, this would be the ultimate justification of our whole journey to the nay-sayers. But my gut was telling me to do it, and my gut has almost always been right. My head and my heart have fooled me a few times, but my gut has always been pretty spot on. Five years later, I realize every bit of that was in my head. No one was judging me. I mean, maybe someone was – but who cares about them anyway?

So, we registered!

I kept kind of quiet about it in the beginning. I guess I was worried about the backlash. But, under wraps, we began to get her ready. During the six months leading up to the showcase, we gradually shared with more and more friends. I was very careful with my words, always emphasizing the fact that I really just saw this as an opportunity to see how she stacked up against other kids her age with the same dreams and talents. I downplayed it as just something fun to wrap around our vacation. After all, it gave us a good excuse to visit family just outside of Orlando that we had not seen in more years than I could count. I said whatever I could to deflect people's questions.

As I expected, reactions were mixed, but very few people fell in the middle. Most were either "all in" or thought I was just some crazy single mom making a completely irresponsible decision. But we were too far down this path to turn back now, so I just swallowed the negative and moved on. I had always told #babybird not to let the nay-sayers bring her down because someone was always going to think you were doing something crazy.

In my own personal experience, the people who question decisions like this one are usually people who didn't have the courage to try something new or take a chance. There was no time like the present for her to learn to deal with the negativity that often surfaces around those of us who choose to take chances in life. After all, she had my blood running through her veins, which meant her life was going to be full of taking chances. So, we just pressed onward without a clue what was in front of us. The one thing we knew was that we both had a "feeling" that we couldn't shake, which meant we had to keep going.

Before we knew it, June was here and it was time to go!

My best friend, Susan, thought it best that I didn't go alone, so she booked a flight and joined in on the fun. She is a bit more conservative when it comes to most things in our friendship. I think of her as the yin to my yang. The peanut butter to my jelly. The ice to my fire. She balances out my crazy and I like to think I spur her on to take a chance or two every now and then. Looking back, I could NOT have done this without her. While #babybird was waiting to go on stage, I was a ball of nerves in the audience. Had it not been for Susan, I would have melted down.

Each evening, #babybird would literally fall into bed from pure exhaustion. I would retreat to the porch to wind down, and thankfully Susan would keep me company. I was not alone. More than anything that week, I needed someone else to see what I was seeing and hear what I was hearing, just to be sure I didn't walk off the plank of Crazytown and ruin my kid's life. While #babybird slept, the porch became my place of refuge. I could release all the emotions of the day with Susan so that I could start with a clear mind the next day. We laughed a lot on that porch those few nights. There is absolutely no way I could have navigated through that without her.

When we arrived, it was more than any of us expected. There were creative people EVERYWHERE and #babybird was at full throttle. I saw a spark and passion that was ten times more than anything I had ever seen in her, even on her very best days. She nailed every single thing she did that week. She took every master class offered and she talked to every person that was willing to hold a conversation with her. She was already mastering the art of networking and had no clue that she was even doing it. I couldn't believe how positive and supportive all of these people were. Strangers stopped other strangers to congratulate them on great performances. Everyone was in everyone else's corner the whole time.

The week culminated in a "call back session." This was a time for the industry executives to call back anyone with whom they wanted to talk to, one on one. It was a tense morning waiting on her "list" but when it came, we couldn't believe what we saw. Twelve of the industry guests wanted to talk to her. My #babybird had turned some heads and I was overwhelmed with emotion.

We saw every single one of them that day and they all said the exact same thing. You live in the wrong city. She needs to be in NYC and the sooner you get her there, the better. She had something special and the only way to truly cultivate it to its greatest potential was to train with the best of the best. And those people resided in NYC. Those were the people working in the business that she had her heart set on someday becoming a part of.

Not everyone was a #babybird fan. There was one person in particular that basically said "You can't wear that dumb flower or no one will ever hire you." Wait, what? My little Mohawk girl had worn a flower in her hair for years. The shorter her hair got, the bigger the flowers got. She was adorable with that giant flower growing out of her head and who was he to tell us that she had to change. I remember looking at her as the words came out of his mouth and she was on the verge of tears. Her flowers were her statement to this world that she refused to conform to the "girls gotta have long hair to be cute" standard. She was a trend setter from that very first flower and she couldn't believe someone didn't like it. That was our first lesson in how harsh this industry can be. That's not to say he wasn't nice about it, but he didn't mince words. He got to the point and he really didn't care if it hurt her feelings or not. He was there to offer practical advice, and that's exactly what he did. Consequently, after arriving in NYC, her agent did recommend she grow out her hair a bit and lose the flowers, so clearly he knew what he was talking about.

One of those interested in talking to us was Roger Del Pozo from The New York Film Academy. I guess you could call this our springboard conversation. He was the first industry person to mutter the words, "move to NYC." At the end of the four days he offered #babybird a scholarship to attend their summer musical theater program for high school kids. It was a four-week program and she could attend the summer before she headed to high school. We could simply put her on a plane and they would "gather" her on the other side, then send her home four weeks later.

I was not ready for anyone to "gather" her in NYC and return her four weeks later. She was a baby. MY baby. There was no way she could handle being in NYC for FOUR weeks without her mommy. I mean, come on, who would remind her to brush her teeth and say her prayers? Who was going to make sure she didn't get kidnapped on the subway? Who was going to make sure her clothes were clean and her hair was brushed? That all sounds funny, but the truth of the matter was, she didn't need me for any of that. I needed HER. I needed her to need me. Sending her to NYC by herself for four weeks was her first step towards independence and I just wasn't ready for it.

But once the words came out of his mouth there was no taking them back. From that moment on, #babybird was going to NYC and there was no one that was going to stand in her way, not even her Mama. When we parted ways with Roger, she told him that we would be in touch to sign up for camp. OK, wait. "We would be in touch?" Who was this kid anyway? Had someone taken possession over her body when I wasn't looking? She was talking like she was forty and I couldn't muster up one single word to contradict her. I was powerless to her determination to get herself to this camp.

The night before we left was the first time that the words "moving to NYC" came out of my mouth. Actually, it came out of Susan's mouth before it came out of mine. She looked at me with the most serious face and said, "Steff, I don't want to tell you what to do, but I think you need to consider moving to NYC." I wish I could say I was stunned or shocked, but I wasn't. She said exactly what I was feeling but too scared to say. A door was opening far more quickly than I ever imagined and I had to decide if I was willing to take the chance and walk through it or not.

The weekend went by so fast. The day we checked out felt like just a few hours after we had checked in. Except as we checked out there were goodbyes, telephone number exchanges and many promises not to forget one another. I was stunned by how these performers had bonded over four days. After living in NYC for five years now, I can tell you, it happens that way with creative people. Their love of performing connects them like magnets. It's one of my favorite things that happens every time she works with someone new. It is truly magical.

We left Orlando and headed to the airport to get Grandpa. Then we were off to the beach for a few days to decompress. So much had happened in just a few days. We had met so many people and my mind was swimming. It took an entire day for #babybird to calm down and for my mind to begin to process the experience.

There were people in this business who thought she was good enough to make a go of it in NYC. What? My kid? My little girl? I just couldn't wrap my head around her surviving in NYC. It was crazy!

July 2nd. That was THE day. It was cloudy that morning, but my daddy loves to walk on the beach, so off we went. #babybird was back to her happy-go-lucky self and I was ready for some R&R. The two of them played ball, jumped in the waves and began making a sandcastle. I watched them for a bit, then decided to see if I could get lost in a sappy romance novel to give my brain a break. No matter how hard I tried, my mind could not stay focused on that book. All I could think about was what to do next. Do we just pick up and move? Could I send her to NYC next summer alone and not have a total nervous breakdown? Was this God opening a door to the next step in our journey or did I simply have blinders on and was seeing only what I wanted to see? Did I need to do anything or just put this weekend behind us and get back to our normal life?

My mind was like a roller coaster. One minute I was high in the sky, and the next it was like that first drop. If you are a roller coaster junkie like me, you know this feeling. You are holding on with everything you have, and your stomach feels like it's going to come out of your mouth as your backside suddenly goes airborne. The anticipation of what was next is almost more than your mind can process and your heart is beating so fast it feels like it's going to pop right out of your chest. There was no sense in trying to read that book. I was not going to retain one single thing I read that day. Too many other things had taken up residence in my mind, and they weren't planning to leave anytime soon.

My daddy must have sensed my unrest because he told #babybird to keep working on their sandcastle and he came over and sat down next to me. He said, "whatcha thinking about, girl?" I stared at him blankly and before I could put the words back in my mouth they flooded out like a rushing ocean. "I think we have to move to NYC." I could hardly believe what I was hearing myself say. But it was too late. I had released it into the universe, and I couldn't take it back. I thought for sure he was going to give me the "daughter, are you really sure this is a wise idea?" talk. But he didn't. He smiled and said very quietly, "You know what's best for her. If you think she needs to be in NYC, I am quite certain you will find a way to make it happen." Without another word he got up and walked back to her and the sandcastle.

Once it was out there, I felt like a giant boulder had been lifted off my chest. I could breathe. I didn't have to make any declarations, but I had spoken it out loud and I wasn't struck by lightning, so there must be something to it. As the clouds rolled in, I gathered those two up and we headed back to the house. In the car I said to #babybird, "Hey, what do you think about moving to NYC?" I kid you not, she jumped so high in the back seat, the car came up off the ground as I pulled out of the parking lot.

She said "Mommy! Are you serious? We are moving to NYC?" She was ecstatic. It was like she had just been given the best present that anyone in the whole wide world had ever received. Her eyes lit up almost immediately, and I knew I had to find a way to make this happen for her.

Here is what you need to hear. ARTS gave us wings. We were 600 miles from home, and those wings were about to carry us into a future that neither one of us could even begin to imagine. Those four days gave us courage that neither one of us even knew we had. The only thing more magical than being with people who love and support you, is being with people who believe in you - truly believe that you have what it takes to do something big in this world.

The team that Kim Myers assembled to help prepare #babybird for this showcase were top notch. Every single person we met was kind, supportive and knowledgeable. They were honest in the best way possible and they made sure she knew exactly what to expect that week. We walked in eyes wide open and left having experienced one of the most amazing four days of our lives.

One of the most important things we learned from ARTS is that there is nothing in this world that is going to make you an instant star. People who get "discovered" have often spent years training and doing every little bit part that was offered to them. One thing led to another, which led to another, which led to another, which led to an opportunity that blew their career open wide.

This business is a marathon, not a sprint. If you do this the right way, each step you take will shine a light on the next. Some steps will be small, and some (many in fact) will feel lateral, like you really didn't go forward at all. Those steps are just preparing you for the BIG ones. The life changers. Her steps started the first time she opened her mouth at four years old and belted Carrie Underwood. Every single coffee table she converted to a stage was another step. Diving into theater headfirst was a big one. Having courage to follow our guts and take a chance on ARTS was the BIG one that changed our lives forever.

I will never forget something that Susan told me that last night on the porch in Orlando. Her exact words to me were, "Steffanie, she was made for this. You were made for this. You have the perfect lifestyle to see where this might lead. Go. Get that dream. And don't look back. I promise I'll always be right here." She was right. I had nothing to lose and #babybird had everything to gain. And, just as she promised, she has always been... right there.

Thanks to my best friend Susan and the team at ARTS, we found our wings - 600 miles from home!

CHAPTER THREE

Two Closets and a Toilet

And that's about it.

The single most difficult thing we have done since making the decision to move to NYC was find a place to live. I had it all worked out in my mind; a cute little walk-up on the Upper West Side (UWS) close to the train surrounded by all the things we might need to live a comfortable life. When Susan, #babybird, and I visited during my first interview adventure, we set out looking for cute neighborhoods that we might like to live in. All three of us fell in love with the UWS. It has character and charm like nowhere else in NYC. It seemed like a reasonable plan. Who knew that my perfect plan would be the first thing that had the potential to derail this entire adventure before it even got started?

Let me give you some data to put things into perspective. I researched a lot, and no one seems to know exactly what the numbers look like, but these numbers are somewhere in the ballpark. And, honestly, what's 100,000 people or so either way, right? NYC's population is somewhere in the 8 to 9 million range across the five boroughs. I found that from 1.5 to 1.7 million of these people live on the island of Manhattan alone. I don't care how you slice it, that's a lot of darn people.

Manhattan alone covers an area that is about twenty-three square miles. When you break that down by person, that's about 70,000 people PER SQUARE MILE - nearly double the amount of people that live in our hometown. Manhattan is also one of the most densely populated cities IN THE WORLD, and for some reason I had it in my little head that we just HAD to live in Manhattan.

Remember, this whole thing unfolded very quickly. From the day we said "let's move," we were here exactly 4 months and 9 days later. (By the way, the original plan was to move a year from July 2nd - not 4 months). I hardly had time to do what I HAD to do, much less do a bunch of research to be "in the know" on all the nuances of the NYC rental landscape.

One of those things that I should have known was how small the actual vacancy rate was in these parts. For the last decade the rental vacancy rate for the five boroughs has been between 2-3%. That means of all the places to live, only between 2-3% are actually available at any given time. All I had to do was find one of those that was the perfect size, in the perfect location, with the perfect rent, and all the perfect amenities that we needed to live a *perfectly marvelous life* for our new adventure. (Two points if you can name that musical!).

And that was my first mistake, assuming I could find perfection within our budget in two days. I was seriously delusional, y'all. Looking back, my delusion was what made this whole apartment hunting adventure far more complicated than it had to be. This would have been a great time for someone to hit me upside the head and tell me to let go of that "it has to be just perfect" mentality. That alone would have saved me a lot of time and energy barking up a tree that I could not climb. I have to tell you, I have yet to meet one single NYer that thinks that everything about their apartment in NYC is perfect, by the way. Except for maybe those people living in the $100 million dollar brownstones in that Upper West Side neighborhood that we fell in love with. (You know, the ones I will never be able to afford.) Their places are probably perfect.

Once the offer letter for my new job had been received I had roughly three weeks to find an apartment, pack up my place - or should I say, give away most of what we owned and pack up just the essentials - and move. I accepted the offer on a Wednesday and was in a car headed to NYC on Friday with complete confidence that I would leave on Sunday with a place to live. I mean, how hard could it be anyway? I was a smart fierce woman. I could do this.

On the way there, I had 11 hours to prepare myself mentally for the drastic changes we were about to experience living in a big city. I knew no matter where we lived, space was going to be tight. I also knew she and I were going to have to come into this with a lot of grace for each other. We had lived in "smaller" apartments before, but we always had decent sized bedrooms so when we began to get on each other's nerves, we could retreat to our own spaces to cool down.

My biggest worry wasn't really the living space. It was the bathroom. She was entering the teenage years and getting ready to go anywhere went from ten minutes to an hour and suddenly involved just the perfect outfit, hair and makeup. One tiny bathroom was going to be a challenge, but I was quite certain we weren't going to find a place that had two, so I resigned myself to the fact that we were going to have to figure it out. One toilet we could live with, but it would sure be nice to have two sinks.

No question, we were downsizing. It was just a matter of HOW FAR DOWN we had to go to make it work within our budget. A studio with room for a double bed and one dresser was NOT going to work. I don't care how amazing the dream was, one of us would not have lived past the first month if we had to be that close all the time. And, I assure you, it wasn't going to be me that didn't survive. Little did I know, that the number of bedrooms was going to be the least of my worries in finding affordable, safe housing for us. I was about to spend three solid weekends in total misery looking for apartments, only to go home empty handed and devastated. All I could find that first weekend, in that perfect neighborhood on the UWS, were tiny little apartments on the tenth floor that looked more like a walk-in closet, than a place where two girls and three cats could live. With each apartment, my heart continued to sink. I know I walked twenty miles that first weekend. Up and down so many flights of stairs that my poor legs cried at the sight of stairs for weeks after. When I got in my car Sunday night, I left empty handed and devastated. This process was so much harder than I could have ever imagined. If I had imagined the very worst-case scenario in my head, it would still be better than apartment hunting in NYC.

The following weekend I would make the long drive again, this time with #babybird in tow. We knew we had to travel light because I was only willing to pay for a hotel for one night, so we packed for the whole weekend in our little backpacks and off we went determined this would be a successful weekend and we would leave excited to move in to our new PERFECT apartment.

Sadly, weekend two ended just like weekend one - empty-handed. When we pulled out Sunday night, we were both crying. It felt like this dream had been so close, yet it was slipping through our fingers like sand through an hourglass, and our time was running out. We easily looked at 52 closets (I mean, apartments) but for one reason or another none of them worked for us. All we wanted to do was find that one little place, that perfect little neighborhood with a vibe that said, "you're cool city people now, and this is where you should be." Unfortunately, our budget didn't think we were cool enough to live in that perfect neighborhood, and no matter how many places we looked at, it just wasn't in the cards for us to live there.

Apartment hunting was the first true test of our willpower to stick to a budget. I had already prepared #babybird that our lifestyle was going to change drastically once we arrived here for good. No more little trips to pick up stuff we wanted but didn't really need. All of our extra pennies were going to pay the rent or see that she had the training she needed to succeed here. It became clear after that second weekend that we needed to expand our area of possibility if we actually planned to have a place before we moved here. Don't get me wrong. We did see some places that we could afford but they weren't exactly what my little heart had in mind. I wasn't about to climb six flights of stairs OR climb over our shared double bed that partially blocked the front door to get to the kitchen. I am not kidding when I say there are apartments here that are barely big enough to fit a bed!

We had spent two weekends here and still nothing. I had to start work in nine days and we still didn't have a place to live. The Peterson Titanic was starting its descent into the great abyss of the deep dark ocean and our spirits were crushed.

This was one of those times in my life where God's favor was more than I deserved. I had totally avoided the idea of a broker despite many people telling us it would save time and find a place that would work for us. My budget was tight, and paying someone more than a month's rent to help us find a place to live just infuriated me, but the reality was that we had wasted two weekends trying to do this on our own and we were still homeless. I had to try something else or we would be paying to live in the back of our rental truck on some random NYC street.

What did one look for in a broker? Heck if I knew! Obviously, their job was dependent on finding people apartments, but we had to find someone who could be on it and make this happen fast. I knew I had no other choice, so I made a call on our way back to WV hoping to arrange to see places the following weekend for our third, and hopefully final, attempt at finding a home.

The first call I made was the winner! I basically told her everything we wanted and all the obstacles we had come up against on our first two visits. I will never forget the words that made my heart drop to my toes, "You have to get out of Manhattan and certainly away from the UWS." What?! My big city dream was crumbling right before my eyes. She could hear the disappointment in my voice and agreed to pull a few places for us to look at just to be sure we had not missed something with our amateur search.

The other challenge I shared with her is that I had less than perfect credit. I told y'all this was going to get uncomfortable - so there it is. I wasn't a perfect money manager. I had always had good jobs, but I was raising a kid on my own and for the last five years I had also been helping my mom with her medical bills. I definitely had some blemishes that would not be easily explained to a potential landlord in a city where there was a 2-3% vacancy rate. Behind me would be someone else that had better credit, rental and employment history in this city, and likely dual incomes to meet the "you have to make forty times your rent to apply" rule that looms over renters in NYC. None of which I had. From the very beginning, my broker voiced her concern that it would be hard to find someone to rent to a single mom from a relatively small town, bringing her 13 year old and three cats to this huge city riding in on their magic carpet of dreams.

I cried myself to sleep more than one night that week thinking I was about to make the biggest mistake of my life and I was dragging my poor starry-eyed kid right onto my very own Titanic voyage that was surely destined to sink. But we had come too far to give up now. There had to be a way.

I'm stubborn. Ask any boss I have ever had. Ask my family. Ask my friends. Ask anyone who has known me for five minutes. I'm stubborn. But my stubbornness, coupled with my determination to not let anyone see me fail, and the kind of faith that is blind to potential obstacles, might have been the trifecta that actually kept us here for the last five years. It was that same trifecta that I needed to push through this mess and find an apartment. There is another thing you should know about me. I'm proud and I don't like to be wrong or told that I can't do something (i.e. stubborn).

No matter what obstacles potential landlords threw at me, I was determined to push onward. There had to be someone out there that would see past what we were on paper and give us a chance.

Weekend three was upon us and we met our new broker. She was very kind and, not shockingly to us, had a history in the theater business. It seemed every person we had encountered thus far had some connection to her dream, instantly felt connected to us, and was willing to do whatever they could to help us.

As she promised, we looked at a couple places on the UWS first. Of course, you already know what happened. There was nothing we could afford or could both fit into. She took us over to the Upper East Side (UES) which was a smidge better, but still not somewhere that we had imagined to be our first apartment. We did find one place that had potential. It was a studio, but as quickly as we applied, someone else came along with rental history in NYC and snatched it up.

Finally, we gave in. We had to get outside of Manhattan. I keenly remember how cold it was that morning. Cold and dismal. Every other time we had visited the city, it had been pretty good weather. As the words came out of her mouth, the chill seemed to be all I could think about. She said, "today we are going to Queens. I think you will see why when we get there." She had eight places for us to see and the moment we set foot in the first place I felt different. It was like warm water was slowly running over my body and I was relaxing. Oddly enough, that was the first peak of the sun that day – AFTER we got to Queens. I know, it sounds silly – but I don't believe things "just happen." And that morning, that sudden ray of sunshine was a ray of hope. We needed something to give us the energy to keep fighting, and this was it.

The first few weren't great. One was a million flights of stairs up. One was too small, (not in my budget UWS small, mind you), but still way too small for us. We breezed through the next few and I realized that we could live in any one of them if we had to. They were safe, bigger, and not horribly far from the train. Things were finally looking up.

We almost didn't see the last apartment on the list. The few before it were completely doable and we were considering applying for all three hoping one would be our new home. But since we were close, we decided we had nothing to lose so we headed over.

The moment we got out of the car I knew. It was the first place that we had seen where I saw a home. It had a cute porch, a little garden out front and it was on the first floor. When we walked in the door, it hit me like a crashing wave. It was big. Way bigger than anything else we had seen. It had decent floors and the bedroom was easily four times the size of anything else we had looked at thus far. Don't get me wrong, it was still small. But it felt like home.

We stayed there longer than any other place. I remember #babybird grabbed my hand as I stood in the middle of the bedroom taking in the space and she said, "Mama, it already feels like we belong here."

I looked at the broker and said, "let's do it!"

The next 24 hours were the longest of my entire life. I mean, longer than that 24 hours of labor that I was in to produce the child who brought us to this place to begin with. I went back and forth with the broker who was going back and forth with the landlord the next morning for two hours. I had resigned myself that if I couldn't do this, then we just weren't meant to move. I didn't say it out loud because I believe that once someone comes out of your mouth, you can't take it back. And the last thing I wanted was to see this adventure end before it even started.

We had to head home not knowing if we had this place or not, which made for a long and somber drive home. Our normal music laden journey was replaced by intermittent tears and a lot of praying. We were both too scared to say much out loud for fear that the universe would conspire against us and we would lose any chance we had of making this little apartment our next home. All we could do was pray and hope that our heart's desires aligned with God's will.

Later in the day the call came from the broker. The landlord had agreed to rent to us, but he had several financial conditions. What? WHAT?!? I had a decent amount of money saved between the generosity of our village and my plain frugalness, but there were so many expenses yet to come that every dollar I allocated to this meant one less dollar I would have in my pocket until I started working and got my first paycheck. Which, by the way, was a whole month after we arrived. I was once again staring down the barrel of blackness. I very quickly felt the Peterson Titanic begin its descent into the abyss. I couldn't shake the sound of Celine Dion belting "My Heart Will Go On" as I envisioned poor Leonardo DiCaprio slip right out of the hands of Kate Winslet and off into the darkness. Seriously ya'll, I have a very vivid mind and it wanders. A lot. Especially when things aren't going so well.

That's when my best friend Susan called. It was like she had a sixth sense that I was in trouble and needed her. She had been my lifeline for many years before the Peterson Titanic set sail for the bright lights of the big city. She saw my struggles, the ones I let no one else see. She picked me up when life had beaten me down. She loved ME, warts and all. She didn't see stubborn, she saw determined. She didn't see fear, she saw courage. She saw ME and that gave me wings that I didn't know I had. She was the only person who jumped right on board the train when we said we were moving. She was like a beautiful bright shining light that blinded me every time I tried to look back. And let me tell you, I tried. But when I did, she would just turn up her light to full brightness so I couldn't see myself anywhere but in this city. Looking backward *wasn't* an option. This was the place that #babybird needed to be and I had to do whatever it took to get her there. Period. See, I'm a mom. I fix things. I had to dig deep and figure out just how to get us there and sustain us for a few years until she was out on her own. Then I could fall apart. But not now. And she knew that. She knew what was in me. She represented safety for me. I knew she was always going to be there, and that was all I needed. She believed in ME. Not that she didn't believe in #babybird's talent, but she was a mom of two teenage girls and she knew first hand a mother's fear of failing their children. (Seriously moms, we all have it - some of us are just louder than others about sharing it). But she also knew me well enough to know that I had the grit we needed to keep the Peterson Titanic afloat. But sometimes, I just needed a little help seeing what was inside of me. She always delivered. Without fail. She was my backbone. My person.

Not to be misunderstood, lots of other people got on our train after the shock wore off and many are still riding this train with us today. But the look on their faces when I told them I had a job and we were leaving in two weeks was priceless. And not in the way the Visa commercial gives you a warm sense of everything is alright in the world when you use your Visa card for some ridiculously expensive adventure that left your child or your elderly parent with that perfect "priceless memory" that money just can't buy. It was a mix of "is she crazy?" and "what is she thinking?" that requires not one word to come out of their mouth. The look on their faces said it all. The first few times I immediately started to justify my decision and name off all the ways that I had thought through this and had planned for every unplanned event that could possibly happen. (After all, I am a planner and I can see into the future and head off any negativity before it hits. Yeah, right.) Eventually I just stopped saying anything and just let them process it. After some time had passed, most of them came back with some level of encouragement and a promise to visit. To date, 104 people have taken us up on the offer to book a room at The Peterson Girls Inn. And I can't count how many more have traveled here on vacation or just passed through making time to spend even just a few moments with us.

Once they were on board, the well-intended advice started coming. People who had been to NYC once twenty years ago, or someone who had a great Aunt once removed that lived 45 miles outside of the city knew everything there was to know about safety on the subway. And let's not forget the people who wanted to tell us how competitive the theater industry is in NYC and her chances of ever making it to the Great White Way were smaller than that first studio apartment I had in Chicago where you could sit on the toilet and cook dinner at the same time. (And, no, I never actually did that, but I could have if the weird need arose. Which could really be good if beans were on the menu that night.)

Alas, I digress. Let's get back to that apartment search.

I needed a boat load of money to get us here. It was the first time I really felt like I couldn't do it, and that the obstacle in front of me was bigger than my little person could maneuver. We never really had money to "throw around" when she was growing up. Living that way in WV was one thing. I had family and friends around. We could always count on being fed one (or four) nights a week by someone that loved us. We had people that were okay if we just showed up so we wouldn't have to be home alone. I had friends that I could drop in on and whisk away on a Dollar Tree or Family Dollar shopping excursion.

The reality was that in NYC, I wasn't going to have someone to drop in on and drag out on some hair brain excursion. I wasn't going to have houses where we could just show up at dinnertime and sit down like we were part of the family. There wasn't going to be summer nights in the park or BBQs. It would just be us. Me and my mini-me. One would think that would have totally turned us around and made us stay in the comfort of our little town where life was predictable. But it didn't. I look back now and realize it actually fueled me even more. I wanted to show #babybird that money should never be an obstacle. If you want something, go get it.

I often hear young people say "oh, we are waiting until we can afford kids to actually have them." The true reality of that statement is that if you wait, you'll never have enough because there is really no way to quantify what you will need. Sometimes you just have to dive in and figure it out as you go, knowing that God is never going to leave you. He's not the "I'll be here for the good times, but when you screw up, well, I gotta go" kind of God. It was the same with this move. I had no clue what we would need, but up until this point I had figured it out. So how hard could it really be? Those words have haunted me more times that I care to admit over the last five years.

But my challenges were no match for God's provision and the support of our village. As quickly as my panic set in, they stepped up. People started to call and say, "We want to say goodbye. Can we meet somewhere for a quick hug?" One of us would almost always leave with a $50 or $100 bill stuffed in our pocket. People came to my house to "buy my stuff" (after all, I was moving out of a two story town house into a dorm room - so I had some serious stuff to unload!) and they would pay me $75 for a $2, ten-year old Tupperware stackable set that had clearly seen better days and likely had at least half the lids that didn't actually fit on the containers because they had been partially melted in the dishwasher. These small "gifts" were mind blowing to me. It's one thing to love people. It's another to step up, dive in and be part of our lives in the most tangible way possible. In a way that I never imagined I would even need.

One of the greatest gifts was from a local restaurant. It actually happened about a month before I even got the job offer. Looking back, there was absolutely NO way we could have made the jump without the help of this amazing family owned Italian restaurant called Paterno's. I had known the owner, Nikki, from various women's groups and "girls night out" events over the years before we moved. She was always such a sweet breath of fresh air. When she walked into a room, you felt good. She made you laugh and feel loved all at the same time. And she had a HUGE heart for helping others and our community in general.

She came to me with an offer. She wanted to host a dinner at her restaurant as a fundraiser to help with moving expenses. She would give us basically everything over cost. Ironically, this happened long before I jumped into the puddle of doom that is apartment hunting in NYC. Remember, I had it all figured out. Every expense was accounted for after all. Except that extra month's rent and the broker's fee. Without even knowing it, Nikki had already filled this huge gap in our plan before we even knew we were going to have a gap. If that's not God's provision, I don't know what is.

She proposed that #babybird would sing a Broadway song before each of the five courses her staff was planning. She would be the entertainment. A cabaret before we really knew that cabaret was even a thing! Plus, this would be one of her last opportunities to sing to her hometown crowd before we hit the road. The restaurant was intimate, and we knew she could connect with these people who had loved us so well for so long.

It was a magical night. We sold nearly every seat in the restaurant and #babybird had the time of her life weaving through tables meeting eye to eye with the people who had loved us more than I think either one of us realized. Everyone from her preschool teacher, to her six grade English teachers, to families from church, and even a few people we didn't know who just thought it looked like fun. #babybird sold a few of her first 'EPs' which had just a few songs that she recorded to take to Florida with us. When we got home, that basket was full of $50- and $100-dollar bills for a CD that had three songs on it. I remember sitting in our house that night holding each other crying with the anticipation of what was about to happen to our lives. God was bowling over every obstacle we came upon.

Susan, that rock of brightness that was constantly catapulting me forward, continued to help me find and solve my "expected" space issues. The night before we left, we went mattress shopping. I had sold my bedroom set in favor of bunk beds and I needed a mattress for my bottom full size bunk. I had never really looked at the cost of a mattress, or at least not through the lens of needing a gazillion dollars to move. With that first price tag the iceberg that I was sure would ultimately sink the Peterson Titanic was right before my eyes in the form of a stupid mattress. I had set aside what I thought was going to be enough. And, it would have been, if I were buying a full-size piece of Styrofoam. But I wasn't. I needed a real mattress. Without hesitation Susan walked up to the cashier and bought me a brand new mattress (which is still on my bed in our tiny little two closet apartment today.) Without so much as a word, she took my measly mattress savings, tucked it into her purse and drove us home. I thanked her profusely, and she just kept saying, "It's a mattress, Steffanie. It's not like I bought you a house, although I would if I could. It's important that you sleep well. This journey is going to be the hardest thing you have ever done, and you won't do it well unless you get good rest." There are still times that I lay on that mattress and allow my water faucet eyes to turn on and let tears stream down my cheeks. That mattress will always be a reminder of the generosity of my village during those last three weeks before we jumped into this adventure.

God almost always shows up for me at the 11th hour. He slides in at the last possible moment when I feel like I have exhausted every single possible way to get something done, but still stand unable to conquer the challenge. On our third weekend trip here, I knew this was it. We either had to find a place to live, or just throw in the towel and give up. Throwing in the towel wasn't an option for me. There were people in my hometown batting against me. Not a lot, but it's a small town and people talk. I knew that when my name came up in conversation some people were just waiting for us to fail. I had to find a way to get us here because failure just wasn't in my vocabulary.

Despite everything the world threw our way to keep us from finding a place to live, we landed in that very last apartment we saw in Astoria, Queens. The one that felt like it could be a home. It was an adorable little one bedroom. Yes, you read that right – we just became roommates – bunk beds and all! The bunk beds were purchased primarily because I truly have no spatial awareness at all. You could tell me the room is 10x10 and I would still manage to show up with a 12-foot bed. In #babybird's first cabaret show she made a joke that "My mom never imagined that she would be living "dorm style" at for - - - I mean ... at this stage of her life." It still gets a good laugh anytime we throw it out there. But, a truer statement has never been made. I had lived in some small places in my younger years, but never did I think I would be living in a dorm room in NYC with my 13-year-old daughter... at forty-something.

It was a super cute place. Super cute and small. Very small. All I remember when we signed our lease was that it was clean and seemed barely big enough for both of us. It felt safe and none of the other 53 apartments that we looked at that didn't work out for one reason or another. Let's be real, I have seen walk-in closets bigger than some of those apartments.

We had the best of all worlds. We were four stops to Central Park. We had a grocery store on the corner with a laundromat right across the street. There was a drug store, a hardware store and a bakery all within a one block radius. Best of all, we were on the first floor. It was magical. The front was adorable, and our little "garden" was filled with every animal you could imagine made out of concrete. We called it our zoo. I think the gorilla and the meerkats were definitely our favorites. Much to our excitement, we even found a nail salon and a beauty salon less than a half a block away. I'm telling you, in NYC that is called a dream.

There was also an unexpected blessing that came with this apartment. People. After about five months of just saying hello as we passed in the hallway, our neighbors (one of which was the son of our landlord) knocked on our door one night to offer us a couple bookcases they were getting rid of and the rest is history. We became instant friends and before we knew it, we were having weekly family dinner and movie nights! This friendship was one of the first things that started to make NYC feel like home. We had people.

Over the last five years, that friendship has grown beyond anything we ever expected the day we signed that lease. We feel more like a part of that family than neighbors or tenants. And as a landlord, they care for us as if we were family, and you can't put a price tag on that. Zach, or as we call him, Zico, manages our building (the old one and the new one) and he has become like a big brother to #babybird. She even worked for him a few summers in his real estate business. One of our favorite traditions the last few years is to invite Zach over to help decorate our Christmas tree.

After a while #babybird started talking about wanting her own room. I couldn't figure out why. I mean, doesn't every teenager want to share a room with their Mama until they are in their early twenties? Yeah, I know, wishful thinking on my part. It was just little hints at first. Then she began to ask. I was comfortable where we were. After everything we had been through just to land in that first apartment, the thought of even considering doing it again made me nauseous every time I thought about it.

Zach often toted #babybird around to showings of his properties just to give her something to do while I was working. Every now and then there would be a two bedroom and she would run home and tell me all about it. Then one day she called me exploding with excitement. Zach had a two-bedroom apartment that was in our price range, a block from the train in a super quiet neighborhood. It ticked just about every box on that list of things that made the "perfect apartment for us" and she knew it. I finally agreed to see it, but I was in no way, shape or form ready to move.

She was right. It ticked all the boxes and then some. Laundry was around the corner with a grocery, a deli and a drug store not far away. The best part of all was the one block walk to the train. It was the one thing that pushed me into even considering moving. No matter what the apartment looked like, in the winter I would be thanking myself for that short walk. Let me tell you, when the wind starts whipping it's pure torture to even be out for a few minutes. Much less fifteen – which was our walk to the train in the first apartment.

Three guys were living in the apartment and were moving next door to a bigger apartment, so this one was going to be ready in about a week. I walked in and for a moment I was frozen. It was small, ya'll. The main living space was easily half of our other apartment. As I made my way back to the "bedrooms" I began to panic. My heart began to race and started to feel nauseous. I knew how important this was to her to have her own space, but these bedrooms were TINY. They were both only as wide as our full-size beds are long. Her room didn't even have a closet. She would have to use the hall closet just to have somewhere to put her clothes. The girl has a LOT of clothes. I imagine wherever we lived I would have had to give up a closet, so she had ample space for her wardrobe.

As we began to talk about how it might work, my heart calmed down a bit. I was not convinced, but she was certain it was the best place she had ever seen. We went home that night and I called Zach to talk about the rent. It was only $50 a month more and they would transfer my security deposit so all we had to do was move. When I called, I wasn't completely sure that I wanted to say yes, but somewhere between hello and goodbye we were making plans to move ten days later.

Do you see the pattern here? I clearly have an issue with jumping in before I have fully evaluated a situation. Thankfully, every time I made a jump on this journey, what was on the other side ended up being far better than where I was before. My gut is clearly more directional than my mind will ever be.

Now that we are settled, I can honestly say that this is a better place for us. We affectionately call it our "two closet" apartment because the bedrooms felt more like walk-in closets when we first moved in. The first few nights were weird. We had been sleeping twelve inches apart for so long, I didn't quite know what to do without her in the next bed. Every now and then one of us will knock on the wall that we share just so we know that we aren't alone. It usually takes me a few weeks to get settled and happy when we move, but this one has been a true labor of love. It has taken us nearly two years to get it just the way we want it, or at least close. It's a cozy safe place for us to retreat to when the city beats us down.

I would be remiss not to mention one of the coolest things to come out of the apartment debacle. With a vacancy rate of between 2-3% you can imagine what the rental section of *The New York Times* looks like. It's pretty massive. Each day they highlight unique rental stories, about people and their journey to make NYC a home. The broker who helped us find our first apartment thought we had just that kind of story and submitted us for consideration. A few months later, they called and wanted to cover our move. I will never forget the title because it truly summed up what this whole journey was about for us. "Broadway Dreams in Astoria, Queens." That was the goal from day one and it was a surreal moment to see our picture and a bit of our story in the *New York Times*.

I don't know how long we will stay in this apartment, but for now, it feels more like a home than just about anywhere we have ever lived. The only thing that could pull us away is a winning lottery ticket that would take us to the UWS to one of those beautiful brownstones. In the meantime, we will just be happy right here in our little two closet, one toilet home.

Love grows best in little houses.
With fewer walls to separate.
Where we eat and sleep so close together.
We can't help but communicate.
If we had more room between us.
Think of all we'd miss.
Love grows best in little houses just like this.

CHAPTER FOUR

But First, High School!

Singin' and dancin' and actin' ... yee-haw!

The word audition just makes my skin crawl. It always has. The thought of standing in front of a room full of people (or even two people for that matter) who are going to determine if I am "the one they are looking for," makes me shake in my boots. #babybird tells me all the time that it is just like me going on a job interview. The thought of her sitting across a desk, talking to someone about her skills and why she is a good fit for a job, freaks her out. Stand her in a room and give her a song to sing, and she is suddenly a canary hanging on her favorite swing just letting her song out for the whole world to hear. My daddy would call this "different strokes for different folks." And, he's right. BUT, every performer will tell you that if this is the life you choose, then get ready for audition after audition after audition. You will have more auditions than you can count. That's just the reality of it. We have been fortunate to become friends with some seasoned performers, and the one thing they always tell us, is you just have to set your mind to the fact that auditioning is just part of the job. It never feels good to be told no, but once you put it into perspective, it gets a little easier to swallow.

We didn't come here blind. We knew that endless auditions were just going to be par for the course if this was the future she chose. But auditioning here was different right off the bat. She didn't know anyone behind the table in these audition rooms at first. In WV, she always knew them and had, for the most part, worked with them at one point or another. They knew what they were getting before she walked in the door. They knew her work ethic and what she was capable of vocally. Here, she was just another number in a line outside the door. (sometimes down the stairs, to the sidewalk and around the block). I could dive into the anatomy of an open call for days, but I need to keep some material for my next book, so we will just stop there.

The first auditions in NYC happened literally one week after she started middle school. I know, right? Nothing like dropping you into the fire without warning. Her first audition was to get into high school. What? Yep, you read that right. You have to audition to get into high school here. Ok, yeah, we didn't realize that was going to be a thing, especially less than a week after we arrived. That's torture of a special kind for a family of planners.

The true magic of this whole story began when we registered her for school (and by magic, I sarcastically mean torture, by the way). The school counselor, who was really anything but nice if we are being honest, handed us a two-inch-thick catalogue listing of all the high schools in NYC. Our job was to go through it and "pick" the places she wanted to "audition" and return it to her. THREE DAYS LATER. People, until that moment we didn't even know there were options. The only performing arts school that we knew existed was LaGuardia, the school made famous by the movie *Fame* and I had not had a single moment to figure out how one goes about auditioning there. We just assumed that coming in November was PLENTY of time to work that out for next year. This was just the first of many missteps we would make along this journey. When I say we got here in the nick of time, I mean it. If we had arrived just a few days later, none of this might have unfolded for her!

As we flipped through this book, we realized there were more than a dozen performing arts schools across the five boroughs that offered some sort of specialized music program. Not every school had Musical Theater, which helped a little in the elimination process. Some schools offered only classical voice, or just instruments, and others offered dance or drama. I would love to say the sorting of the schools happened quickly, but the reality is it took me nearly 24 hours straight to just get through the book. If you know me at all then you know my Type A personality shines its brightest when there is something to be organized. And boy was I glowing! We finally narrowed it down to about ten schools. "Country come to town" over here was terrified at the thought of my little #babybird traveling by SUBWAY to high school every day - alone! So, I set out to ride the subway to each one of these schools so I could see for myself what her journey would be like each day.

It made me feel better to say that I didn't want her to ride the train, but let's face it, how in the world did I think she was going to get to school? Walk!? Not hardly. After riding to each of these schools I quickly eliminated about half of them from the list. Any neighborhood that made my Mom heart beat much faster than I preferred was eliminated immediately. (Yes, I was that crazy overprotective mom who was terrified to let my kid ride the subway to parts unknown.) That left us with eight schools, one of which was an all-girl leadership academy, just in case she didn't get into any of the performing arts schools.

Her first audition was the following Friday, so she had about five days to prepare once we turned in the list to her counselor. There were four more after that, but the last one was the only one that really matters. We arrived at the Professional Performing Arts School knowing we had missed the first round of musical theater auditions and she was signed up for a vocal audition. The vocal program was mostly classical training, but something was better than nothing. Luckily for #babybird, if she landed a spot, she had classical training in her background so it wouldn't be totally foreign. Despite what that two-inch handbook told her to prepare, she proudly walked into her audition with a Musical Theater song.

There are so many details about that day, but this is my book, so I am going to tell you MY side of the story. Maybe someday she will share all the things that happened on her side, but for now, you're stuck with just mine. As soon as we walked in the door and got her checked in, she was pretty much swept away with a group of kids. I had no idea how long this was going to take or where she went, but I was directed to the auditorium where all the other hopeful parents sat on pins and needles. Some were in clusters talking, others (like me) were sitting alone just taking in everything that was around them. A parent stood up and told us what was happening and that our kids would come back down when they were done, etc. Then she pointed out the vice principal, who was responsible for overseeing the four major performing arts programs for the school: dance, drama, musical theatre and vocal.

I have never wanted to be "that mom" that thinks my kid deserves special accommodations and I certainly didn't want to start out on that foot with this school. We knew the moment we walked in that this was where she belonged. I had heard people talk about the "instant connection" they felt, but I had never really felt it myself. Until that day. I hadn't even talked to #babybird to see what she thought, but I knew. I remember sitting in my seat praying, "God, please let this be it. Please let this be it."

Before I even knew what I was doing, I stood up and walked over to the vice principal. I am certain these auditions take their toll on administrators as much as it does directors who are casting a show, so I tried to be as calm and collected as possible. I introduced myself and very quickly shared that she had missed the musical theater auditions and asked if there would there be a makeup audition. I read in that giant catalogue that some schools did make-ups, and some did not, so I had to at least ask. His face went very stern and he said, "Well, that depends. Why did you miss the auditions?" There it was - the teacher face. I imagine being an educator himself, he was preparing to hear the sob story about the dog eating the audition form and that's why we missed it. Lucky for me, my answer seemed fair. "We just moved here a few days ago," I said. His face softened a little, and he responded, "let's see how things go today and go from there." In my most charming southern voice possible I said, "thank you very much," and I turned and walked away quickly as not to say anything else that might make me look like a fool.

Shortly after, #babybird returned. She had made a friend and they were both all smiles. She said, "It went amazing, Mom. So much fun." Finally, I could breathe. The whole reason we moved here was for this and she seemed truly pleased with her audition. We chatted with the young lady and her mom and walked out the door thinking we would hear something on March 1st, just like all the other kids.

The process of determination is essentially an algorithm. You audition for the schools you want, rank them and turn in your sheet to your middle school counselor. You get an audition ticket, show up and audition, and then wait for the process to work. Every student is asked to provide a myriad of supporting documentation as part of the "application process," which included transcripts, immunization records, letters of recommendation, etc. Seriously, for someone who did not grow up here, this felt an awful lot like applying to college. Once you audition, the school ranks their preference and it goes into this big "computer" and kids are placed and notified sometime in early March. Because these are public schools, there are many factors that actually go into this process. It's really not as easy as audition, we want you, and you're there.

As we walked to the train, she began to spit out all the details as if she was on a ticking time clock and she had T-minus two minutes to get it all out or she would blow up like a stick of dynamite! I'll skip the tiny details, but the gist of it was this. She walked in and they asked her to sing. She got about halfway through her song and they stopped her. The gentleman behind the desk said, "Did you audition for musical theater?" With a big smile on her face she told him that she didn't because she just moved here." He said, "Let me see what I can do to help you, but let's go ahead and rhythm test you." Our chances of getting into that Musical Theater program had just doubled, people! It was my turn to get excited and hurriedly tell her about my 9.5 second conversation with the vice principal. As if the cutest boy in school had just walked by and given us a second look, we both squealed like 13-year-olds, jumping up and down and hugging. You would have thought she had gotten the letter of acceptance right there on the corner of 48th Street and 8th Avenue.

We both knew the worst part was yet to come - the waiting. She didn't want to go to any other school. She wanted to be in a smaller school and PPAS was just that. And, as we learned later on, it was packed with a ton of kids working professionally in theater, film, television, etc. These were her people. About a week passed and no news. Then, it came. Early in November we received a letter from the school. It contained a piece of paper that simply said: *Musical Theater Dance Call Back* - with the date, time, location.

I think we both were a little stunned because it took us a minute to realize she was being called back for THE MUSICAL THEATER PROGRAM!!! We still don't know who crossed her over to the Musical Theater department, but someone was in her corner! These people had already seen hundreds of kids that day, and they had already seen hundreds of kids the weeks before. She was just one little girl and it would have been so easy to just "forget" to pass her along. But they didn't, and here we were, marking our calendars for one week from that day for her call back.

This is where it really gets fun, ya'll!

The following week, I was just sitting in my little office on 56th and Madison working away. I had already told my boss I needed to leave early to get her to an audition the next day and had planned the timing of the whole day to be sure we arrived early. I finished my lunch and reached for my planner (yes, a paper planner... shush) to mark something down. Except as I looked at my calendar, I realized the audition was actually TODAY! In an instant my heart sank into the pit of my stomach. I had misread my calendar. I looked at my watch praying that it was 11:30am and not 12:30pm, but alas it was exactly 12:30pm and auditions started at 1:30pm. I immediately ran to my boss who looked at me and said "Why are you still standing here? GO!"

I grabbed my things and sprinted out of the office processing in my brain how to get her there on time. Unfortunately, I knew that nothing short of time travel was going to make that happen. I called her middle school and they basically said she can't leave without you PHYSICALLY standing in the office signing her out. I couldn't send a fax, an email or anyone else. (Remember, we are two weeks into our adventure, so I hadn't even had time to find an emergency contact yet!) I talked with everyone from the secretary to the principal. And they just wouldn't budge. I remember her principal saying, "Ma'am, this isn't the South. We take student safety much more seriously here in NYC." OK, if I had not had the other crisis to deal with, this Southern Mama would have jumped on a train and taken this guy out. How dare he insinuate that we don't think kids' safety is important. But at that moment, I had bigger fish to fry. I had to go get her out of school and to this audition, so off to the train I ran.

In route I called the audition site and spoke with a sweet young man. I wasn't in complete panic mode yet, but I was pretty close. Trying not to pant, I told him the Cliff Notes version of my complete failure as a mother. He very sweetly told me not to worry. Just get there as soon as we could. When I get mad or nervous or panicked, my accent comes out - in full force. I am pretty sure this kid hung up that phone, not quite understanding what had just transpired, but that the woman on the other end was slightly crazy.

Thankfully, the train came into the station just as I crossed through the turnstile. I hopped on the N train and just started to pray. As it hit the first stop in Queens the conductor made an announcement that this train was going express and skipping four stops due to track maintenance. Now, some of you may have seen my Facebook posts about the good ole' MTA. The subway system and I are rarely friends. It has taught me a lot about life (see chapter entitled Train Logic), but it's been a love-hate relationship from day one. Not really knowing what else to do, I stayed on the train and frantically began to Google her school and how to get there. We were still in the "there is one way to get to work and school, and one way to get home" mode. We were nowhere near competent at navigating the subway system, much less when a train unexpectedly goes express. It took me all the way to end of the line - Astoria Ditmars Boulevard. My panic level was increasing rapidly. It was 1:20 at this point and she was essentially already late.

Then a stroke of genius! A cab! It's not that far, I will just take a cab! I know, stroke of genius seems a bit much, but remember, where we come from cabs aren't necessarily the safest mode of transportation. Now, in the "Bologna Week" chapter of this book, we will learn just how tight money was for us that first year of living here. Two weeks in meant I still hadn't gotten a paycheck. We were flat broke. We were broker than broke. I didn't even have enough money to take a $10 cab to her school. I was the worst mother in the world and in my mind the Peterson Titanic had begun its descent to the bowels of failure, and I could do nothing to stop it.

I stood on that train platform in tears. I texted her and told her she would just have to wait and take the train right after school into the city. It was nearly 2:00pm, so she only had twenty minutes until the bell rang. At this point she is already thirty minutes late and we weren't even out of Queens yet! The plan was that I would meet her at 42nd Street and we would RUN to the audition. It was the middle of the day, so of course, trains were few and far between. Luckily, I was still above ground when she texted back. Another blow. She didn't have a subway card with her and the one at home didn't have any money on it. (Refer to paragraph above about being broker than broke.) I could hear my heartbeat as if someone was standing right next to my ear walloping a giant bass drum. Ba-boom. Ba-boom. Ba-boom. I was defeated. Plain and simple. Some days are just too big for one person and today was my day. Epic Mom fail and all I could think to do was cry. She said, "Mom, let me see if I can borrow one. I'll ask a teacher. Get on the train back into the city and I will text you."

SHE is the resilient one of this duo. Sometimes she does have a little of her mother's tendency to go down the black hole of disaster, but not often. She was going to find a way to get into this city. Even at 13, she realized the importance of this audition. The train came and I felt like I was moving in slow motion, tears streaming down my face and my head hanging low. We had made it two stops when my phone rang. The N train stays above ground for six stops before it tunnels in for the stretch under water between Queens and Manhattan so I still had cell service. Before I could even say hello this little voice screamed, "I got $3 for a Metro card. I am running to the train, Mama!"

I hung up with a smile in my heart. We were late, but we were going to make it. I hopped off the train at Broadway so I could make one more frantic call to let them know we were coming! As I was dialing, I felt a sudden pang of sadness. What if they told me too bad, don't bother? What if her being late because of my mistake cost her the whole audition? Performers know "early is on time, on time is late and late simply isn't acceptable in this business." At 13, that was still a lesson she was learning, and probably would need another five years to really let it sink in how important that beginning on time was to every aspect of her life.

Since the day we became a two-some, certain things were always in the back of my mind that I knew she had to learn. It wasn't fishing or how to change a tire. It was life skills that would serve her well no matter what career she chose. It was life lessons that I learned the hard way. I had to teach her to be responsible; be on time; always be over prepared; plan ahead; always be the one who offers to stay late and be the hands that helped clean up. I wanted her to be a good human no matter what her situation. Maybe most important, I didn't want her to ever feel like she "needed" someone else to take care of her. I wanted her to be strong, self-sufficient, and dependable. When she finally met the man of her dreams, I wanted her to marry him because she loved him and couldn't imagine doing life without him, and not because she needed him to pay the bills and fix flat tires.

My mind began to spin as I dialed the number. The same sweet voice that had listened to this frantic mom try to explain that SHE had totally screwed up gently said, "It's okay. Just get here as soon as you can." Before I could even hang up, the phone beeped and #babybird was calling again. My heart sunk. Something had gone wrong. When I said hello, all I heard was the sobs of the sweet little voice of my girl. Fighting against every obstacle, she had come up against another one. In NYC it is $2.75 to ride the subway, and she had $3.00. But she didn't have a Metro card and to get a new card, you have to pay an extra $1.00, which means she actually needed $3.75. At this point, anyone would have understood if she just gave up. She was a kid and the world was just clobbering her, as if it would do anything to keep her from this audition.

This was MAYBE the third or fourth time in her life where I literally heard her melting down. The desperation in her voice was cutting though my soul and there was nothing I could do but listen. I had no advice for her. I was as broken inside as she was. After all, this was all MY fault. I had messed up the calendar. I had caused this whole debacle and her heart break was all my fault. Why in the world did I think for a single moment that we could do this life here in NYC? Before I could say another word, she said, "I'll call you right back," and she was gone. I couldn't even get an OK out before she hung up.

Less than a minute later, the phone rang again. "Mama, I made it through. I'm getting on the train!"

The only thing I could think to say to her was "did you run under the turnstile without paying?" I know, not exactly the motherly concern I should have shown in that moment, but I had seen kids get picked up by the police for doing the exact same thing. In my mind I couldn't process any other way that she would have gotten through. She didn't give me a chance to follow up my ridiculous assumption before she blurted out, "The little man in the ticket booth let me go! I'm running to the train, see you soon," and again, she was gone. Problem solved, so there was no reason to keep talking!

What I learned later is that she used her most precious power of persuasion to convince him to let her through... tears. Yes, she cried. Right there in the middle of the train station she had a total breakdown. "I just need to get to my mommy! She is in the city and I don't have enough money!" Bless his heart, the last thing he wanted was to see a little girl crying for her mommy. He said, "go, go, go," and opened the door and off she went. I told you she was resilient and if a meltdown was the ticket through the door, then a meltdown was what she was going to dish out in that moment of desperation.

I hopped back on the train, and for the first time since this nightmare started over an hour ago, I felt like I could breathe. I felt a peace I had not felt all day that everything was going to be fine. I just had to get her and run like heck to get there just as fast as we could.

I made it to 42nd Street, raced through the train station and found her waiting at the stairs for me. When I saw her she clearly had been crying. Who wouldn't have cried at this point? The biggest audition of her little life and her mother had made a debacle of it. But, at that moment I didn't have time to do any consoling. It was time for Supermom to spring into action. We barreled up the stairs as fast as we could. When we reached the top, we were met with yet another unbelievable obstacle. The moment we stepped out of the train station, the heavens literally opened up and rain began to fall as if we were walking under a massive waterfall. We looked at each other and for a moment we were just in pure shock. Really, God? A massive rainstorm RIGHT NOW? Neither one of us had an umbrella. We clearly weren't New Yorkers yet, because if we were, we would have checked the weather and popped an umbrella in our bags.

If you remember, #babybird had come straight from school. Her school had a pretty strict uniform policy and since it was getting cooler she had worn her school t-shirt, hoodie, sweatpants and tennis shoes. Hardly acceptable dance attire, but it was either that or dance naked and barefoot. But that wasn't the only problem with her wardrobe. This cotton blend sweat suit was now drenched and heavy. The water just soaked right in and she looked like an honest-to-goodness drowned rat.

When we finally arrive at auditions, the God of all creation chose to ease our minds in the most amazing way possible. The door flew open and the SWEETEST little lady said, "You must be Hannah! Come on in ya'll!" Wait. Did she say "ya'll?" And with that, the worry just washed away. We had made it and we had been greeted by this fiery redhead that sounded just like us. I will never forget how kind her eyes were. Before I knew it, they had scooped #babybird up and taken her upstairs to the "unclaimed dance clothes and shoes box" and suited her up for a dance audition. All I had time to say was "I love you" and she was gone.

Toni Noblet was the name of that woman who I am certain God himself planted at that door to welcome us. She could see the terror in my eyes, that "I am sorry, I tried" look that transcended any words I might have mustered up at that moment. She gently escorted me into the room which was FILLED with other kids. But they all looked normal. Hair pulled back, appropriate dance clothes and shoes, and moms and dads who didn't look like they had been dragged through a mud puddle.

With a sense of calm that made my heart jump back into normal rhythm, she leaned against a wall a little out of the way and she began to talk about anything other than this audition. I tried twice to "explain" and "apologize" but she simply said, "It's okay, Mama. Stuff happens. We get it." And with that, we began to talk about making biscuits and gravy and all things Southern. I learned she was from North Carolina and, if #babybird was accepted, she would be her freshman tap teacher.

After what felt like five minutes, but was actually more like thirty, my little bird came out of the stairwell in clothes I had never seen and ballet shoes that were a size too small, smiling. Yes, she was smiling. Whatever happened in that room made her happy. She had missed the call back completely, so they had her join in a ballet class. Ballet? I can't tell you how thankful we were that we didn't know that before arriving. I am certain that might have been the one thing that tipped us over the edge after the hurdles we had jumped to get to this point. #babybird had taken only a few years of baby ballet when she was 5 and 6, and one more year when she was in 6th grade and that was it. A ballerina she is not. But she pulled it out. Somehow, that little non-dancer danced her way through that class.

You already know how this ends. She spent her four years of high school at the Professional Performing Arts School in the Musical Theater Department. Two hours a day, every day, she studied her craft and continued to fall in love more and more with performing and telling stories.

The moral of this story? Never stop pushing forward. No matter what the obstacles are, no matter how hard the rain pours, push onward.

Giving up just isn't an option.

CHAPTER FIVE

Bologna Week

How low can you go?

For many years, the last week of the month has been penned "bologna week" in my house. Also affectionately known as "mac n' cheese week," "clean out the pantry week," and sometimes "we are fasting week." Regardless of what we called it, it was the last week before I got paid, and in the early days that meant we lived down to our last dime, sometimes even pennies.

I had a running joke with a friend from home to see who could drain their bank account down to the lowest amount without overdrawing. I think she won with thirty-two cents left on one payday. We would even send photos back and forth with our bank balances as proof. On some level I think it helped us both realize that we weren't the only ones living on fumes at the end of the month. I told y'all I was going to keep it real, and this is real!

There have been many, many valuable life lessons that she and I have learned over the last five years, but I truly believe that learning to manage a budget is right up there at the top for her. Several years before we picked up and moved, I started doing budget dates with her every January. My WV pastor, Matt Santen, had been doing this for years in his family. This was truly a revelation for our little family. It was like someone had taken the blinders off and suddenly I had a kid who started to think about money in a whole new way. Not to say that she still didn't ask for things she didn't really need, but it became much easier for me to say "no" when it wasn't in the budget. She knew the budget. And if it wasn't there - it just wasn't there. No fuss.

I am a single mom, living in one of the most expensive cities in the world with a kid who has this dream that isn't a cheap endeavor. Voice, dance and acting lessons - oh my! (Yes, you should say that to the tune of lions and tigers and bears - oh my! It's just more fun that way!) Dance clothes, shoes and let's not forget the injuries! Not to mention if you are going to pursue theater, you gotta see theater. And, theater ain't cheap here, people! Sure, we see a lot of stuff on Broadway. But we also see a lot of stuff off Broadway and even off-off Broadway. As a matter of fact, some of our most memorable shows have been the ones that never made it to Broadway. It only took a show or two for us to realize there is truly something intimate and magical about a smaller theater.

Now, I am not going to lie, the dream is Broadway. Anything else is amazing, but her soul won't rest until she stands on that stage. For her, there is nothing quite like a live audience. It's electrifying. She needed to see shows. She needed to see shows like you and I need air. It was a sort of survival tactic for her. When life was great, we celebrated at the theater. When life was tough, we recovered at the theater. When there was nothing else to do (which truly was not often) we would fill our time at the theater. Theater is a part of the fabric that makes her who she is, no doubt about it. But her desire to see shows did not always align with my budget. She always wanted to see more shows than what I had dollars to buy tickets for. There have even been times when she has been presented with the question "groceries or theater." Wanna guess which one she chose? Yep, theater. Every single time. If this kid had her way, we would be in a Broadway theater every night of the week!

I know, you are reading this and laughing in disbelief. Your mind is saying, "oh, she's exaggerating! Look at Facebook, those girls are always out and about going to shows and all kinds of stuff. They have plenty of money. After all, she works in Manhattan and they make so much more money there than most other places." You are partly right. We DO see a lot of shows. We

DO spend a lot of time doing fun outings in this city. Who wouldn't if you had the privilege of living here?

In the beginning, I had a standing rule - one big ticket a month which almost always ended up being a Broadway show. There have been a few months where she has chosen something different, but for most of the sixty months we have lived here, we have seen at least one show a month. Do the math. That's a crap ton of theater in five years.

Now, clearly, I love theater almost as much as she does, of course in a very different way. I'm just fine sitting in the audience, and even better when she's the one on stage. I can't count the number of times during a show I watched her inch her way up until she was literally on the edge of her seat. It would not have surprised me in the least to see her jump out of that seat and head straight for the stage. It's that deep of a love for her. I am pretty sure there are only three things she loves more than theater. Jesus, her Mama, and sprinkles. In that order.

BUT - if she was going to go down this path, she had to come to terms that nothing about this career was going to be easy, or cheap. The reality is she will always be hustling to her next project to be able to pay the bills. I secretly pray every day that one of us will either hit the lottery or she will hit it big and we won't have to worry quite so much about getting by. But, my soul rests in the comfort that no matter what, this kid will be doing exactly what her heart desires, and that will make every moment of the hustle worth it for her. She will tell you that she's a-okay living in a tiny apartment, eating Ramen noodles twice a day, as long as she gets to do what she loves.

One of the zillion house mottos we have is "have train pass, will travel!" And let me tell you, we do. I like to envision there is a little man in a remote office of a high rise building somewhere in Manhattan and his entire job is to pull my monthly bus/train travel records. Every time he pulls it, he buries his head in his hands and says "Yep, we lost money on those darn Peterson Girls AGAIN this month. How in the world do they ride like a family of five?" When someone says to me, "you girls are never home," I smile knowing that means we ARE living every ounce of this dream both on and off the stage.

Ask anyone who has lived here even for a short time and they will tell you, once you navigate away from the tourist stuff, NYC is a city of fun, free adventures. We spend many lazy afternoons in the park or taking ferry rides to Staten Island just to soak up some sun and fresh air. We love to dilly-dally (that's a technical term, by the way) through street fairs in the summer or just walk our favorite neighborhoods on the UWS. One of the things we love the most is to be out in this city when it snows! There is nothing more magical to us than walking the city streets during a light snowfall at night.

There were times where we were down to one roll of toilet paper and I threatened her within an inch of her life to use more than one square. (By the way, you have no idea the pride I have for the levels of frugality that we brought into our lives to be able to keep this dream going these last five years!) Have you ever heard the words "house poor?" It means you stretched your budget so thin that you have no money left to enjoy life because you spent it all on a mortgage or a rent payment. While everyone else is out having fun on the weekends you are at home looking at your ridiculously expensive leather couch trying to convince yourself that the couch was worth losing your entire social life. I assure you, we are right there with every other New Yorker, paying more for rent than I ever paid for a mortgage, but that was not going to be our life! We happily sit on our $300 couch, in our tiny little apartment, so we can spend every free moment we have running around this city like we have nothing but time and an endless supply of money! (Which we don't, but it's sure fun to run around like we do.)

Sure, it would be great to have a fancy UWS address, with a little more space, maybe a door man, a second bathroom and laundry in our building. (That's the dream, people!) But the reality of our story is that we couldn't have had all those things even if we wanted them. We also came to realize early on, that we didn't need any of that. What we needed was safe, convenient and just big enough for two girls and three cats.

One of my favorite revelations from #babybird was just a few weeks after moving to the city. Clutter just makes my skin crawl and long before NYC I had a heavy hand when it came to cleaning. We had always had larger places and cleaning was usually a good half day event for us. I was a little firm on not living in a pigsty, so I used cleaning days as bribery in order to do fun stuff. Clean the house and we can go out. Don't clean the house, and you sit in your room all day. You choose. I'll happily curl up with a good book and read the day away while you sulk because you didn't clean the toilet.

We had spent about an hour picking up, mopping, etc., when she bounced out of our bedroom and said, "I could get used to this small apartment living, Mama. It only took us an hour to clean the whole house and our bathroom at home was never that clean!" That was one of the first moments where I knew we were going to be just fine living in smaller places.

If I am being honest, frugality has really always been my life. I have been a single Mama for most of her life, so I have always had to pay close attention to the household budget. It's taken me a long time to be okay with laying my challenges out there for the world to see. And, truly, there has been no greater challenge than finances. I am just like every other single Mama out there who does everything they can to be sure her kid(s) never go without. #babybird often felt the pinch, don't get me wrong, but she knew that if it was in my power to do something for her, I would. And that was enough for her.

This move took frugality to a WHOLE NEW LEVEL, friends. I tell people all the time, God knows how to stretch a dollar farther than my mind can even begin to imagine. And, I can back that statement up with proof! He has done it every single month for the past five years without fail.

The reality of living this new frugality wasn't really about the big things, it was more about the little things. Take laundry for example. I lived with "four outfits a day Sally" in my house and as soon as one bag had been delivered to the laundromat, another had already begun to multiply. To be fair, once she got to high school, she did wear a set of dance clothes every afternoon, which made for a small pile of extra laundry all on its own. As much as I would have loved to have her "re-wear" them, my cleanliness meter just couldn't do it. But that didn't account for the third set of clothes that she would wear AFTER school, because you can't put back on the clothes you wore all day. I mean, come on, mom. That's gross. And of course, a new pair of PJ's every night.

After safety, my next geographic priority was to be sure to live in close proximity to a good laundromat. Let's be real here, I was not about to schlep 25-30 pounds of laundry more than a block or two. It just wasn't happening.

In the beginning it sounded so big city to say we "send our laundry out" but it truly was the most economical, and fastest, way for us to get it done. By the time we paid for it by the load, AND bought detergent, AND bought fabric softener, we could pay someone else to do it for us for less money. Plus, we could find something else to do that was a whole lot more fun than watching the laundromat TV for three hours every weekend. It was a win on all fronts!

The other challenge we faced (and continue to face) in our

budget is food! It definitely takes a massive amount of planning and organization to ensure that we aren't wasteful. We had a half size fridge in our first apartment, so we could usually only fit maybe four- or five-days' worth of food at one time. One of the budget balances I mastered living in WV was buying in bulk. Listen, I would buy enough toilet paper to last three months! Not here, man. And, don't get me started on the size of the pantry. Literally, I had a two-door cabinet on the wall and that was it. It held a bottle of vinegar, three cans of tomato soup and a box of crackers. (Ok, that's a slight exaggeration, but you get the idea - it wasn't a walk-in closet like I was used to back home!) It was actually kind of funny that first year or two because I was in the grocery store more days a week than I wasn't. After a while. I began to realize that I was seeing the same people doing the same thing - just picking up a few things.

Why does this matter in terms of our budget? Well, let me tell you, it costs far more in the long run to buy four little ketchup bottles than two family size ones from Costco. And besides buying multiples, groceries are expensive here! I always try to add in my head what's in my cart before I get to check-out. My Mama used to make me do this when I was a kid to work on my math skills. I would have to tell her what I thought before the cashier started. If I was close enough, I would get a reward.

The first time I shopped here I did my usual ritual of adding in my head as I went. I wasn't a third of the way through my list and my grocery budget for the WHOLE MONTH was blown. I stood in that teeny-tiny aisle (and I do mean tiny - some barely big enough for one cart to fit down the aisle!) looking at my meek little basket trying to decide what we could live without - milk, eggs or cheese.

It was a very long time before we were able to add an "eating out" line item into our budget. Even today, we definitely rein in how many meals we eat outside our home. Just like "theater or groceries" we often play "theater or eating out" when there happens to be more than one show that we MUST see in a month.

There is no way I could share our food and budget woes without our favorite eating out story. We had lived here for about three months. I had been squirreling money away to take us out for a nice dinner. There was this great little Spanish place just off our train. It had a giant pink car coming out of the roof and it always seemed to be busy. I figured it must be good if the place was always packed, so we made a date and went out to dinner.

When the waitress brought the menu, I realized we might be in trouble. Not financially, we had plenty of money for dinner. But the menu was in Spanish and neither one of us spoke Spanish. #babybird had her required two years, but that was not nearly enough to navigate this menu. We tried to decipher what words meant. We even Googled a few. But when the waitress returned, we were as confused as when she set down the menu. We tried to have her help us, but her Spanish was excellent. English, not so much.

Like every other decision in our lives over the last year, we just jumped. We picked something that we thought we would like and took a chance. Worst decision of our lives. She brought us pig's feet. PIG'S FEET, people. I had saved up so we could have a nice meal to celebrate our three-month anniversary, and she brings us pig's feet. In case you're wondering, we didn't try the pig's feet. We shared our sides and ate every single chip in the bowl and left. To this day when we walk by that restaurant, we stop and giggle to ourselves remembering that night.

I remember the first time we went to Taco Bell. (I know, I live in NYC and I eat at Taco Bell. Just shush.) We got pretty much the same thing we got back home, and our bill was around $12-$13 for both of us. When the man behind the counter said, "that's $29 Ma'am," I literally laughed in his face. I thought he was joking. $29 for a couple tacos and a Mexican pizza? You have got to be kidding me!

No matter how hard we tried, we just couldn't win at the food game for the first several months. But I am happy to report that we finally found our rhythm and our food woes seem to be in the past. We still calculate in our heads in the grocery aisle, but we also get to treat ourselves to dinner out more than once a month; and it's always something other than pig's feet.

Besides food, I think our greatest sacrifice has been clothing. WE LOVE CLOTHES. All of them. From pretty skivvies to warm cozy jackets. We just love clothes. At home we had a pretty nice stream of hand-me-downs, some of which were things that had never even been worn. #babybird has always been a bit of a fashionista so she gratefully accepted anything tossed her way. She has an eye for throwing things together and comes out with the coolest outfits. But we weren't in Kansas anymore, people. Our budget was tight, and our space was even tighter. In that first apartment we shared one small standard size closet and piled the rest of our clothes onto storage shelves that I dragged all the way from the basement in WV.

It was time to get creative and introduce the girl to the art of resale and vintage shopping. She was like a fish to water. Every single time we passed a resale shop she wanted to go in and she ALWAYS found some bargain that she just couldn't live without. We even planned a few "hit as many stores as we can in one day" outings in search of new places and cool pieces. And let me tell you, there are a few (spoken with sarcasm) resale shops around here. In every neighborhood there are multiple places tucked away with treasures just waiting to be found. And we were the girls to find them.

Having her embrace that was key for us. She knew we had to put our pennies where it mattered most and if she could supplement her wardrobe with some resale pieces, then she was all in. Now our problem was where to put all our finds!

This particular part of the journey was very hard for me because it affected her more than me. We sometimes didn't schedule voice lessons and wore holey ballet tights to save some pennies. More times than we can count we uttered, "I'm sorry we have plans" when we were invited out because we didn't have enough money to make all of that happen and keep the lights on.

And you know what? We are okay. Missing a few voice lessons didn't ruin her chances of making it to Broadway. She is as determined as ever and working towards it every single day. When I step back and really look at the financial struggles we faced learning to live here, I feel blessed that we made it. Every struggle has made us appreciate what we do have so much more.

We live in the coolest city in the world.

She is performing regularly and meeting really cool people who share her passions.

I am working on Fifth Avenue with a Central Park view doing something I love.

We have a sweet little apartment in a safe, beautiful neighborhood that we love.

We have community.

We have access to the things that fuel her soul.

We have SO MUCH to be thankful for.

The old saying "money makes the world go round" is never more relevant than when you live in a place like NYC. It takes a whole lot more in return for a whole lot less to make a life here. So, we had two choices. (1) Let money control us and haunt our journey focusing on what we don't have or can't do; or (2) learn to live within a new budget keeping our eyes on the prize. The reason we came here to begin with. Broadway.

This move made me realize that every so often we should ALL stop and take an inventory of our lives. Reevaluate what we have and where we spend our resources and our time. Life is about experiences and when you keep your eye on the experiences that life lays out for you, your soul feels different. It's full. And that is a feeling I never want to leave my body.

This is a hard place to live. It does take a lot out of us emotionally, financially and physically. But we are living our dreams, and when you're living your dreams, all the other stuff just doesn't seem as important as it once was.

CHAPTER SIX

City Livin'

One day at a time.

Culture Shock. That's what everyone says when we tell them we moved here from West Virginia. "Gosh, I bet this was a big change for you girls." Ummmmm, duh? Of course, it was! There are no front yards to play capture the flag, or creeks to catch crawdads. There are no open fields without rules. (Yes, I might hold a little bitterness towards the "rules" of the parks here.)

But I imagine when someone born and raised in this city makes the move out to the 'burbs, they have pretty much the same feelings - just in reverse.

It truly is nothing like West Virginia.

That's good and bad, I guess. It has certainly tested our resilience. We are stronger, more adaptable girls because of it. Living in a big city means making game time decisions. Train goes express, you adjust your plan quickly. It starts to rain unexpectedly, you have to find shelter. A friend calls just as you are headed home from work and has just landed theater tickets for the night and wants you to go. You make it happen.

This city has worn us down at times. So much so, that after about a year, we really started to question if we actually had the chutzpah to make it here. You know the song, "If you can make it there, you'll make it anywhere?" That song is 100% truth. NYC is like nowhere else in the world. Lifelong NY'ers are probably rolling their eyes about right now, but for these two girls, this was a major life change.

I remember when we first moved here, a now dear friend said, "you need to give yourself a break from the city every now and then. You will need it, trust me." This was at a time when we still had on our rose-colored glasses (with sparkles on the edges) and thought that nothing could ever possibly make us not want to be in this city every second of every day. Yes, we were those people who moved here from a faraway land completely enamored with everything we saw, from flower shops on the street corners to rats in the subway. Everything was new and exciting. At least at first.

You know what comes next. Gradually the novelty wore off. The weather changed and the grind of city life kicked in. I remember being in a cab about a month after we arrived. If you know me then you know I strike up conversations with anyone I can. The driver was a middle-aged man who called himself a "lifelong NY'er." When I shared that we were relatively new to the city, his first words were "if you can make through the first winter, you'll be fine. Just be prepared. It's dismal here in January, February and March. The winter will feel like forever. But spring will come, you just have to be patient."

Boy, he wasn't kidding! Dismal doesn't even really completely cover what it looks like here those first few months of the year. We were NOT prepared. Let's make that clear. There was not one single cell in either of our bodies that was ready for what we had jumped into with both feet. We came here with blinders on thinking that everything would be just like it was on the few visits that preceded our actual move. I now know that those few long weekend trips we took between May and October when we were job interviewing and house hunting were the times that fairy tales are made of. The sun was out every day. The air was crisp in the morning and warm, but not hot, in the afternoons. There was no rain or snow and we weren't carrying a heavy school bag or purse to weigh us down. The sounds of the city were invigorating, not overpowering. The scents from the food trucks were wonderfully new. They were blissfully perfect weekends.

But the fairy tale was just about to get a little dose of reality thrown in to keep us humble. The first couple weeks were great.

We were still on such a natural high from taking the leap we could have cared less how many coats we had to wear when the temperatures dropped. We lived in NYC and that made everything else seem trivial. Thankfully, reality set in at a nice slow pace. We weren't bombarded with every little thing that makes NYC a crazy place to live all at once. It began with a few cooler days. And then a rainy day or two. But nothing we couldn't handle. It was still cool to take the train to work and into the city for our exploring excursions, even when they were packed full and running late.

Looking back, I can now laugh at what unfolded in the following months. I said it once and I will say it a million more times, if I had actually known what I was getting myself into, I probably would have never considered making the move. God is cool like that. He knew we needed to be here, and He knew this control freak would never have jumped with my eyes wide open, so he kept me just enough in the dark to get me here then let the city unleash its madness on us one season at a time. Apparently He knew before I did that once we got here, I would work it out somehow. He was right. I did. It may not have always been pretty, but I worked it out, nonetheless.

Let's start with the weather. I don't like the cold. At all. Not even a little bit. I am good so long as all I need is a sweater or a light jacket to take the chill off. Once you cross over into full-on winter jacket weather, I shut down. Next to walking our legs off, this was definitely one of the hardest physical adjustments for us. That and climbing subway stairs. Five years in and my legs STILL burn about five steps from the top. When I hit the pavement at the top of the stairs it's like winning a medal for this girl. (I know, that's the point in which I should walk my happy self into a gym. I will. Someday.)

Around wintertime this meme floats around Instagram and Facebook and I share it every single time I see it. It says, "why do I live in a place where the air hurts my face?" Why would anyone do this willingly? Because Broadway is here, and this entire journey rested on that dream. When winter is at its worst and we have on three layers of clothing, ginormous coats and 90% of our faces are covered by a hat and/or scarf, we remind each other - this is where Broadway lives, so this is where we live. It doesn't make it any less cold, but the end somehow justifies the means, so we just keep pushing onward.

Another magical part of NYC is that snow stops pretty much nothing. Unless we are headed for a record-breaking blizzard, or the coldest temperatures in over a hundred years, NYC still marches on. Because we bring a little bit of sunshine wherever we go (Thick sarcasm here!), our first winter marked one of the worst snowfalls NYC had seen in YEARS. It was a bona fide blizzard. The whole darn city shut down. No Broadway. No Subways. No Driving. It was the calmest I have ever seen the city. Residents were told to stay home, the snow was coming. The boroughs usually see slightly more accumulation than Manhattan. Which can be good and bad, but that night, it didn't matter. We were all getting walloped and it didn't matter where you lived.

It snowed, and snowed, and snowed, and snowed. We topped out at about 18" on our little porch. You already know I hate the cold, but let me tell you, my first apartment was often colder inside that it was outside. Old building. Old windows. Knowing we weren't leaving the house for at least a day, we dragged my mattress into the living room floor and just camped there because the living room was the warmest part of the house.

Before we turned in for the night we had to bundle up and go for a little late-night walk in our new city. No cars, no loud music; just the soft sound of falling snow. The roads were completely covered and pretty much empty. The snow was piling up by the minute. We galloped down the streets making snow angels as if we were little kids out on a snow day! We haven't had that much snow since that first winter, but we have had our fair share of snowy days, even a few school cancellations. But for the most part, we get up, even in the snow, and go about our daily life. There were many days that walking home was like using a Stair Climber that had the resistance turned all the way up. Wind blowing IN YOUR FACE and fresh snow piling up on the ground giving you a workout without ever having to set foot in a gym.

I have come to be okay with the winters, but rain, that's a whole different ball game for me. The only time I truly dislike living here is when it rains. I can deal with the cold, but I hate being wet. And I really don't like riding the subway because it always smells like a gaggle of wet dogs. Plus, we are tasked with dodging rain as it pours down through cracks in the ceiling of subway stations that were built back when dinosaurs roamed the earth. I am STILL not used to the rain and I am honestly not sure I will ever be, because I just don't like to be wet. Period.

And, in NYC when it rains, you are going to get wet. There is just no way around it. There are puddles all over the place that either soak your shoes or cause a nice splash as the cars drive past. People don't use umbrellas responsibly here, so you are constantly dodging the water that runs off of THEIR umbrella as you try not to get your eye poked out by some tourist who has no spatial awareness. Now, you can do things to minimize the level of wetness. Like rain boots for example. Helpful, unless they sprout a hole while walking in a thunderstorm. Yes, I know, what is the likelihood? Very good if you're me. Rain jackets are helpful, too. But you better be sure it's truly waterproof, because if it's not, you're going to spend the first hour of your work day drying out. Do not ask me how I know this. I just do.

In the early days we didn't look at the weather much. It was cold, so we put on a coat, what more did we need to know. We needed to know about precipitation, that's what.

Did you pack a hat to wear home once the temperature dropped to ten below? Did you pack an umbrella just in case the heavens opened up JUST as you came up from the subway? Was there even the SLIGHTEST chance of either one of these? Because if there was, then you had better be prepared for it before you left the house, because once you left, there was no turning back. There simply wasn't enough time in the day to be going to and from home in between work, school and rehearsals. So when you set out that morning, you better have everything you needed for the day. You were either prepared or not. And if you weren't, you were either freezing or wet - sometimes both.

One thing was for certain, when you weren't prepared, the city was prepared for you. Street vendors are on every corner, all winter long, selling hats and scarves. You would be fine, as long as you were willing to drop $10-20 each time you forgot your hat. Umbrellas were not as plentiful on a day-to-day basis, but when it actually rained, five guys with 100 umbrellas stuffed in their milk crate cart suddenly appeared. Like the chimney sweeps from *Mary Poppins*, it seemed like they came out of nowhere. One minute nothing and the next minute there were three of them right in front of you. Which was great, but by the time I realized I didn't have an umbrella, I was soaked and not really sure what good it would do to buy another one. We have accumulated quite the collection of $5 umbrellas around our house from all the times we forgot to check the weather. Rookie mistake for living in a big city that we rarely make now.

The only thing that was harder than the weather was transportation. If you follow me on Facebook or Instagram, then you already know how I feel about this. It sucks. It's never really been consistently good since arriving in our sweet little city. It has definitely had swings of decent, and an occasional good, but mostly just a "royal pain in the arse" as my daddy would say. I won't dive into the things I learned while riding public transportation, because that is a chapter all its own, but I will tell you that my lack of direction was an adjustment that I have never really been able to overcome, even five years later.

I have ZERO sense of direction. Less than zero if that's even possible. In all fairness, a small amount of my train anxiety was the fear of getting lost and not being able to figure out how to get myself found again. Remember, I was forty-one when we moved here - clearly not a spring chicken. When I say I think I can do anything I set my mind to, I mean it. But with age, things don't come quite as quickly as they did when I was 20 years younger.

Everyone said, "you'll get the hang of it, it just takes time." Clearly they overestimated my internal compass because my sense of direction has not improved one single bit with time. I still come up from the subway at LEAST once a week and have no clue which way I need to walk. Google Maps saves me practically on a daily basis. But even with Google at my fingertips, I sometimes end up backtracking because I took a wrong turn. Whenever people visit, I always say, "As long as we are with the GPS with fur (#babybird), we will be fine." (You get double points if you can name that musical.) This child can literally get us anywhere. It's astonishing to me to watch her maneuver us to places we have never been. I can't even begin to explain how I bore this child that has such a keen sense of direction when I have none. I would love to say I gave her mine in the "baking process" but the fact is, I never had any to begin with. I guess I should be grateful that one of us has it or we might still be trying to figure out how to get anywhere.

My favorite transportation fail story happened about two months after we moved here. It was a very cold Friday night in January. I worked late and didn't head home until after 8pm. At that time of night you are almost always going to find a seat. I got on at the last stop in Manhattan and the train did its usual acceleration under the water and into Queens. And, by acceleration I really mean the conductor releases the train like a bat out of you know where and then comes to a screeching stop once it hits the first station in Queens. I swear there are some days that I KNOW we fly off the rails. However, on this particular evening, the train seemed to be moving slower than normal into the station. Then, we came to a complete stop. We sat for probably 20 minutes, mere feet from the platform, before the conductor came over the speaker to tell us that this train would not be going further and we would have to exit. Exit the train? What?!?! I had lived here all of two seconds and he wanted me to get off the only train that I knew would take me home? How was I supposed to get home?! It was too far to walk, and it was cold. Very, very cold. As I walked down the stairs to the street I saw the amoeba of people moving towards buses. The problem was, I had never been on a bus a day in my life. Did I really want my first bus experience to be on a dark, cold night when I didn't have a clue where I was? My vote was a definite no.

Against the objection of my checking account, I decided I was going to take a cab. Except, by the time I made up my mind, there were no cabs to be found anywhere. I waited for about five minutes and decided I needed another plan. My feet were freezing and to make matters worse, my phone was on 3%.

We had two family rules about moving around the city when we first landed here. First, you text me when you leave home and when you arrive at your destination. Second, if you are walking and it's remotely dark, you must be on the phone with someone. I don't care who, but you better find someone before you start walking. While this was MY mom safety net at the time, I realized later that she was actually keeping relationships from back home alive with every phone call.

If my phone died, I was cut off from her in a city that was still very foreign to me and I was breaking my own family rule. If you have teenagers then you know - once you break a rule, they will never let you forget that one time out of a million that you messed up.

With no cab in sight, I quietly said to myself, "Okay transportation Gods, I can play this game, I will just take an UBER." We have a car service budget each month, but we really try to only use it when the weather is just nasty, or when we have our hands full, or if it's just super late and commuting home seems unbearable. I am not lying when I say I must have hit the "find your ride" button 10 times and as quickly as it said, "your ride is on the way," they cancelled. At this point, I was starting to panic. How in the world was I going to get home?

Faced with what felt like no other option, I was just going to have to get on that bus and see what happened next. At this point, I can sense #babybird's panic setting in with every text. She was home alone and I was trying to limit communication to preserve my battery. I knew I had to be a big girl and get on that bus and trust the good Lord above to do the rest. By the time I got to the next bus, it was already packed. Two other trains had dumped off what seemed like a bazillion more people who all needed to get home and that bus was their only way.

I was the last one on before the driver abruptly closed the doors. As the bus pulled away, I began to try to make out what was around me. Had I seen any of this before? Was anything even remotely familiar? About 2 minutes into the bus ride I pulled my phone out to tell her I was on the bus, hopefully headed home. Wouldn't you know, it was dead. So now I was taking my first bus ride, on a very cold dark night, with no cell phone service and absolutely no clue where I was. Great, I had just set myself up to be the subject of the latest episode of Law and Order SVU.

As the bus moved along, I started to think things *maybe* looked familiar. Then all of the sudden I knew where I was, sitting right in front of The Dollar Tree on Steinway Street. At that moment I knew I was on the right path to my apartment. The question now was, where do I get off? How close would the bus get to my house? Would it suddenly make a turn and I would have to get off on some dark street corner? My instincts kicked in and at the very next stop I jumped off and started to walk. At least this way I knew where I was and how to get home. It would be a cold walk, but rather cold than lost.

There was a lot of traffic that night and as I walked, I pretty much kept pace with that bus. Every two blocks it would stop and people got off. Yes, you guessed it, I got off the bus WAY too soon. But the best part of the whole story is that the bus stop that I should have stayed on for was one block from my house. Boy did I feel like an idiot. As I walked into the house, #babybird wrapped her arms around me as if she hadn't seen me in years and began to cry. She was scared. When she finally let go, I looked at her and said, "Well, at least we know how to ride the bus now." She wasn't amused.

That night taught us both two things. Number one, never leave without enough battery to get yourself home. Our deal was that we were always connected. While it may seem silly to some, being out of touch for that forty five minutes, me worrying about how I was going to get home, and her not able to get updates from me, taught us a lesson that we have not broken since that day. And, number two, when in a new city, learn how to use the bus before you actually NEED to know. It just works better that way.

People ask us all the time if we miss having a car. If you had asked me anytime during the first six months of living here, I would have said yes. No question. Ask me today, and you will get a very different answer. Yes, public transportation can be a nightmare here. But I don't have a car payment or a monthly insurance payment. My budget doesn't include money for gasoline or maintenance. I don't have to get my Metro card inspected each year to get my new registration sticker or take it in for regular oil changes. If I need a car for a day, I just rent one. In the meantime, I'm happy maneuvering the city on a train, or a bus, or a ferry. Despite my angry posts, it's better than dealing with a car any day.

Aside from the weather and moving around, the city has taught us some things that will make anyone who hasn't had any experience living in a city chuckle. For example, you can't possibly survive here without good bags. Purses, duffles, backpacks. Every time you leave your house you have crap to carry. For the majority of high school #babybird's friends called her "The Bag Lady" because she showed up to school with more bags than the normal person takes on vacation. On an average day she had her purse, her lunchbox, her dance bag and her backpack. And, they were full of very important stuff that she absolutely needed. (Sense the sarcasm here...) Talk about schlepping, this kid schlepped.

Let me clarify, not just any bag will do. At least not for us. It has to fit nicely over your jacket and stay up on your shoulder. It can't be too big, and it can't be too small. It has to hold all your stuff but be big enough that if you stopped for anything while you were out, you had room to stuff something else in said bag. I'd venture to say we have had enough bags in this house to move a small family from one continent to another.

After bags comes shoes. We love shoes. I mean we LOVE shoes. At one point in my life, way before a NYC apartment and this kid of mine, I owned over 200 pairs of shoes. Yes, all at one time. Now, some of them were 10 years old, but if they got worn once a year, they qualified as part of the collection. After about three months here I quickly realized that we were going to wear out shoes faster than I ever could have imagined. And, sadly, many of my favorites were not practical city shoes.

We walk roughly 3-4 miles on an average day between getting to and from work and just maneuvering around our day. On the weekends, we have been known to walk 8-10 miles and not even realize it. Before NYC my dad would always say, "you girls need another pair of shoes like you need a hole in the head." He was right. We didn't NEED shoes - we WANTED shoes. #babybird used to respond by saying, "Grandpa, you know shoes make the outfit." He would just chuckle at her knowing there was nothing he could do to change that kid's love of shoes.

I have found one little spark of happiness as a result of burning through shoes so fast. We get to buy new ones much more often because we "need" them, not just because we "want" them. Call it what you want, but I will justify my shoe habit anyway I need to, thank you very much.

If you have spent any time with us here in the city, you have heard us grumble about some random tourists who have messed with our day in some way or another. They stopped dead in the middle of the sidewalk to gawk at a tall building, or a pack of them slowly sauntered down the street standing five wide so no one else could pass by. Or our most frustrating times are when groups of people get on the subway acting like total fools because they think that's how NY'ers act.

Let me make something clear. True NY'ers are amazing. They are pretty much the nicest people you will ever meet. They are the ones who help strangers standing on the corner who are clearly lost. Or the couple staring at the subway map with great determination but have no clue how to get where they are going. A real NY'er is always happy to help. If you encounter a NY'er that's not nice, there is something more to their story. I have been that NY'er a time or twenty. Most often it's because I am trying to get somewhere and you, sweet visitor, are on vacation and not in a hurry. I have most likely been delayed by some dumb train and I am now running down the street desperately trying not to be late. So ... when I rush past or say "excuse me" in a less than overly friendly tone, just move aside and let me through and I will quickly move on about my day.

But this is a tourist city. And some days we have to just dial it back a bit and remember we live in one of the most amazing places on this planet. I guess I hope to always be a tourist to a certain degree. I want to come up from the subway on a random Tuesday night and feel overwhelmed with emotion at the pure blessing it is that we get to call this place home. I can't begin to count the times we look at each other and at the exact same time say, "we actually live in NYC." I want to get lost every now and again so we have funny stories to share with family and friends who are terrified to ride the subway.

These things I know for sure. We will continue to scour tiny little neighborhoods looking for new places to explore, restaurants to patronize and history to learn. We will go to every Thanksgiving Day Parade, because we can. We will celebrate the lighting of that giant tree and try to get our silly mugs on TV, because we can. We will ride the Staten Island ferry and adoringly look at Lady Liberty on the way over and on the way back, because we can.

While city living has definitely worn us out at times, it has given us life in ways that we continue to discover the longer we live here. We never want to tire of the magic that NYC tucks away on its streets just waiting to be experienced. We never want to take for granted what a privilege it is to live here.

We have had more than a hundred visitors either stay with us or pass through for lunch or dinner. Some people we knew, others were simply friends of friends who just wanted to connect. It's been quite a blessing to have these little bursts of home. When you visit, we will take you to Times Square because you should go there at least once in your life, but we promise you it is our least favorite place to hang out. It's actually our least favorite place outside of the five boroughs, too. I know, that's where Broadway lives. We should love it there. Well, we love Broadway, but that's about where the love for that little nucleus of Manhattan ends.

After you have explored the tourist attractions that NYC is known for, we hope you will let us take you off the beaten path to some amazing little corners of this city that are engulfed by "locals" enjoying everyday life in this truly extraordinary place.

By the time this book is in your hands we will have celebrated five years in our fair city - FIVE event-filled, sometimes scary, challenging years. In the last two years, things have really blossomed for both of us. I think the best part of celebrating the last five years is that we both feel like we can finally call ourselves real NY'ers. And that's worth everything to us.

The ARTS

The event that started it all, and the people who have cheered us BOTH on from the moment we made the decision to move. They believed in us before we even believed in ourselves. They have celebrated each win (no matter how big or how small) and continue to encourage us to reach a little farther tomorrow than we did today.

Hannah Jane and Kim Myers of ARTS International

Kim Myers, Hannah Jane, Mama and Rick Myers
during Kim and Rick's first NYC visit after the move.

High School

High school was a time of great accomplishment and a time of great challenges for #thepetersongirls. Hannah Jane spent her four years of high school in The Professional Performing Art School nestled in the heart of Times Square. What a beautiful experience it was for me to see her grow into her craft day after day after day. The icing on the cake was the many extraordinary relationships we both developed that will stay with us forever.

First day of Senior Year, September 2019

Hannah Jane with her acting teacher, Greg Parente
Senior Showcase, May 2019

Hannah Jane with
Vice Principal Karime Flores

Hannah Jane and her BFF, Keron Medina

Hannah Jane and Jeff Statile
Director of the Musical Theatre Program

Musical Theater Excellence Award

Hannah Jane with her Grandpoppy Jim

Hannah Jane and Mama
Graduation Day, Times Square

Photo: David Rosen

Cabarets

One of the coolest discoveries for Hannah Jane was the art of cabaret. Until moving here, we didn't even know cabaret was a 'thing,' much less something that she would grow to love.

On My Way was Hannah Jane's debut solo cabaret and arguably one of the most exciting nights of both our lives. In September 2018, friends and family from as far away as Florida, and as close as three blocks away in NYC, came out to support her as she took the first big step towards her dreams.

Less than six months later, we were doing an expanded version of this show in our hometown with TWO sold out performances. While every performance is special, doing this in front of the very people who helped launch us into this incredible journey was remarkable in every way.

Her sophomore show, which was presented at Birdland Theater in January 2020, *Lady Legends of Broadway*, celebrated the women she has looked up to since she set her sights on a performing career. These extraordinary women represented not only some of the best shows Broadway has ever seen, but also what you can achieve when you put your whole heart into something you love.

Hannah Jane
Lady Legends of Broadway Cabaret, January 2020
Birdland Theater
Photo: Stephen Mosher, Broadway World

Hannah Jane, Jon Weber, Lauren Cohn (known to her friends as Coco),
and Mama; or as Hannah Jane calls them: The Dream Team!
Preparing for *Lady Legends of Broadway* Cabaret

Hannah Jane and Lucia Isabelle Schwartz
Lady Legends of Broadway Cabaret

Hannah Jane and Kristy Cates
Ladys Legends of Broadway Cabaret

Jon Weber and Hannah Jane

Coco Cohn and Hannah Jane

Hannah Jane and Marc Tuminelli

Hannah Jane and Mama

Coco Cohn, Hannah Jane, and Eugene Ebner
during her first interview for *Broadway World*
to promote her first solo cabaret show, *On My Way*

On My Way Cabaret, September 2018

The Dress

Walker Deaderick, Hannah Jane, Barbara Deaderick (our Ninja mover)

Hannah Jane and Tom Koontz, one of our biggest WV fans!

Kimberly Hudson, Hannah Jane, Kayli Hudson
On My Way Cabaret

On My Way Cabaret

Hannah Jane paying tribute to her Nana
On My Way Cabaret

Hannah Jane with Adam Bryan at The Alban Arts Center
at her WV Cabaret *Where It All Began* (February 2019)
which was an extended version of the *On My Way* Cabaret
presented in NYC in September 2019

Hannah Jane and Coco Cohn, *Where It All Began* WV show.
This photo is worth a thousands words. It's the best picture
I could have ever painted of the sweet relationship these two share.

The extraordinary team we assembled for the *Where It All Began* WV Cabaret.
Jon Weber, musical director; Coco Cohn, director; Hannah Jane;
Brandon Willard (who was Hannah Jane's sixth grade Magnet music teacher!),
drums; John Ingram, bass.

Hannah Jane and Mama

Hannah Jane

Hannah Jane in Times Square
following her *On My Way* cabaret

Larry and Adela Elow endowed The Mabel Mercer Foundation Mabel's Babies Award. Hannah Jane was second place winner.

People

At the very center of this entire journey is the glue that has held us together these last five years. People. Family, friends, teachers, mentors, neighbors and fellow performers just to name a few. There are truly no words for how important these people, and the relationships we have developed with them, have been and continue to be in our journey! These are just a few of the MANY people that have been with us through all the fun! I can't imagine for a single second not having these amazing humans by our sides.

Hannah Jane and her agent,
Craig Holzberg of Avalon Artist Group

Hannah Jane on the day she signed her first
contract with Avalon Artist Group.

Hannah Jane and Kristy Cates
Hannah Jane's first time backstage at a Broadway show
Finding Neverland, 2014

Hannah Jane and KT Sullivan, her Cabaret Mama

John Fricke and Hannah Jane
after the 30th Anniversary New York Cabaret Convention

Kristy Cates (Hannah Jane's first voice teacher and her 'Mama Diva')
and Hannah Jane at the *Lady Legends of Broadway* Cabaret

Hannah Jane and Jon Audric Nelson

Hannah Jane and Dasha Bradshaw
Winners of the 2019 Global Peace in the Streets
United Nations Award

Hannah Jane and Zach "Zico" Hassan, our first neighbor

Hannah Jane and Grandpoppy Jim

Hannah Jane and Mama
on The Gilmore Girls Tour of CT

Hannah Jane and Mama

Hannah Jane paying tribute to a fellow WV
girl (Jennifer Garner) in a NYC train station

Hannah Jane sporting her New York Film Academy swag

Photo: A Class Act NY

Shows

Over the last five years, Hannah Jane has had the opportunity to embody many cool characters and work with some extraordinary directors in pursuit of this dream. With each show, she made new friends, grew as a performer and made me extremely proud of her dedication and commitment. At every opening night, I was reminded that the hard parts of this journey were completely cancelled out the moment she set foot onto that stage. She was in her element and happier than I can even put into words.

Hannah Jane as *Annie*
August 2008

Hannah Jane as *Miss Hannigan*
Middle School, May 2015

Hannah Jane in *Be Aggressive*
Junior Play at PPPAS, June 2018

Hannah Jane in *Bring It On*
Broadway Workshop, May 2015

Hannah Jane as *Toria* in *Blood at the Root*
Senior Play at PPPAS, June 2019

Hannah Jane as a player in *Pippen*
Broadway Workshop, April 2017

Hannah Jane as *Sister Mary Lazarus* in *Sister Act*
Broadway Workshop, May 2019
Photo: Broadway Workshop

Hannah Jane singing at *Holiday Musical Magic*
December 2019

Hannah Jane as *Skylar Quinn*
World Premiere of *PsyKidz*
January 2019
Photo: A Class Act NY

The Lincoln Center

On October 30, 2019, Hannah Jane was invited to be part of the Mabel Mercer Foundations 30th Annual NYC Cabaret Convention held at Jazz at The Lincoln Center. The evening honored Hannah Jane's musical hero, the great Judy Garland and was hosted by the amazing John Fricke and Klea Blackhurst. To be invited to be part of this glorious evening was truly a dream come true for Hannah Jane. During the middle of her performance, she was surprised to be honored as the recipient of the 2019 Julie Wilson Award, which is presented each year by The Mabel Mercer Foundation and Linda and Peter Hansen, to an up and coming performer. To say the night was magical is an understatement. I don't think either one of us will ever forget a moment of that entire evening.

Hannah Jane singing at the
30th Annual New York Cabaret Convention
October 30, 2019

David Myers (uncle), Mama, Hannah Jane, James Myers (Grandpoppy)

Hannah Jane sings at the
30th Annual New York Cabaret Convention

Klea Blackhurst and John Fricke
Presenting Hannah Jane with the Julie Wilson Award
at the 30th Annual New York Cabaret Convention

Hannah Jane and KT Sullivan

Mama and Hannah Jane

The Move

On November 9, 2014, we left WV with our dear friend, Barbara Deaderick, driving our packed rental truck, me following right behind with our three cats tucked away and absolutely terrified. It was a long trip, but nearly 14 hours later we pulled into NYC to begin our new life. Looking back, there is absolutely no way we could have made it without her! She got us there, helped us unpack, and navigate to the essentials in our neighborhood. I thank God every single day that I didn't have to face those first few days alone. And, I think we are all thankful for the sweet little man from the corner supermarket who loaned us a grocery cart to help make the half block walk from the rental truck to our apartment (at 11pm at night mind you) with our boxes just a little bit easier.

Grandpoppy Jim saying goodbye to his girls

The Move Crew
Leaving WV on November 9, 2014

Our first kitchen
Astoria, Queens

Barbara Deaderick
Yes, we moved in with a grocery cart!

Our first apartment

Our garden zoo

Mama and Hannah Jane
Hannah Jane's graduation party, May 2019

CHAPTER SEVEN

Toothpaste

Not just for brushing your teeth!

Toothpaste.
We all need it.
We all buy it.

Well, except The Peterson Girls.

When we prepared to make the leap to NYC, somehow my dad decided that we needed to not ever have to buy toothpaste. Yes, you read that right. Toothpaste.

We pulled out with about ten tubes packed in our toiletries and we have yet to buy a single tube. People, that's FIVE years of toothpaste that I didn't have to buy. That's five years that I never had to worry about running out. You know exactly what that feels like. You wake up, stumble to the bathroom knowing that if you breathe on anything between the bed and the bathroom it will spontaneously combust or wilt into a pile of unrecognizable mush. And that's just what happens when you breathe on "stuff" - don't get me started on what that breath could do to actual people. You reach into the medicine cabinet to pull out the tube which, by the way, had you paid attention last night, you would have realized you had rolled the tube as tightly as possible to get that last little bit of paste from it. But, you didn't. Honestly, the fact that you got anything on your toothbrush was a miracle.

Why the dissertation about toothpaste, you ask? Running out of toothpaste wasn't something we ever had to worry about. As trivial as that sounds, it was one less thing I had to build into our already tight budget. But it was so much more than that. It was just one of the many small ways my daddy always made sure we had what we needed. Living ten hours from "his girls" was very hard for him. As much as we appreciated the toothpaste, I think his heart swelled a little with each tube knowing he was playing a role in our journey. He saw it as giving me one less thing to worry about. It was a sign of his love for us. And it has continued. Every couple months a care package shows up with a tube or two. At Christmas, our stockings have a tube for each of us. When he visits a tube or four end up on the counter before he leaves. We joke about it often. But never once has it ever just been a tube of toothpaste to us.

The toothpaste was just the beginning for us. Not long after we arrived in NYC a small box appeared in our mail one day. We opened it to find a full box of hand and feet warmer packets. And let me tell you something, that first winter we needed those. Our FIRST winter in the Big Apple was cold. Remember, we had the worst snowstorm to hit the city in years. It was also one of the coldest winters in many years. So, yes, hand warmers were a welcome arrival.

There are many things about living in this city that can wear you down. Standing on a train platform that is outside in the dead of winter is one of them. Naturally, our first apartment was closer to the above ground train than the underground one, because, you know, why not? I guess it was essential that we conquered all the hard stuff early on so when the sweet stuff started happening, we were all the more thankful. Seriously, remember I said the hard stuff. This was right up there for me. I was old when we got here. At 41, I hadn't waited outside for a train on a cold snowy morning in 25 years and my body was just not happy!

It took us a day or so to figure out who they were from. I love a good surprise care package just as much as the next person, but I wanted to say thank you to the kind soul that was worried about the warmth of our hands and feet. With a little investigating, we connected the dots that led to my sweet friend, Chrissy Preservati. I met Chrissy when #babybird was little through a bunch of theater, performing, dancing kind of stuff that both our girls were part of. Chrissy and her daughter, Julia, were kindred spirits and whenever we were together there was always lots of laughter. Chrissy was one of the first people to join team Peterson girls when we shared our plans to move. These little hand and feet warmers were just a little something to remind us that we weren't alone or forgotten. Someone far away was paying attention to our lives here in NYC and just wanted to lighten our load a bit. The beauty of this particular gift was that every single time we used one, we had a sweet moment of gratefulness for this simple gift, much like toothpaste.

Speaking of things to keep us warm, we were blessed not once, but twice with 'warmth' from other friends. Debby and Herb Peters lived across the street from us when we first moved back to WV. #babybird was just about two years old and was quite the spunky little monkey. We grew to love them so much that they became known as our Bonus Grandparents - Nana Debby and Grandad. Thankfully, they have kept us tucked in the fold of their family all these years. During that first winter, everyone from home seemed to tune in to the national news and weather a little more than normal. Anytime anything having to do with NYC made the news, we would get check-in calls and texts to be sure we were ok. (Yet another reminder of how well we were loved by our WV village.) Deep in one particular cold spell, Nana Debby called to 'check in' on how we were doing with the cold. Were our coats warm enough? Did #babybird really HAVE to walk to school in the cold? She had been following my funny posts on Facebook of #babybird and I, and how we were weathering the cold. One showed us so bundled up neither of us was recognizable even to those that had known us our whole lives. We assured her we were well layered and that the walk to school wasn't as far as it sounded in my dramatic Facebook posts. (Drama runs deep in this family.)

Before we hung up, she said, "I'm sending you a little money. Please go get you girls some leggings." Let me tell you, this little blessing was welcomed with open arms. It was cold that winter. Freezing cold. I often get asked if it's colder here than at home. Most people assume it's much colder, and sometimes it is. But my standard answer still holds true. It's about the same temperature most of the time, but we are out in the thick of it here. Back home we had a nice warm car to get us to school, work and everywhere in between. Let me tell you, there is nothing like walking down a cold street with the wind whipping under your coat to wake you up on an early morning walk to the train to get to work. Looking back, this was a little way that Nana Debby and Grandad could love on us from afar. They worried about us and they wanted to help take something off my plate. In this case, leggings. I was going to have to buy those leggings no matter what. Just like the toothpaste, they served a great purpose in our lives at a time when everything was new and what we thought we knew was in a constant state of change. It was something small by most people's standards. But for us, it was mammoth. Those leggings made such an impact on our daily lives that first winter - and even into the second and third. I actually think I still have one last pair of what we fondly called "Nana Debby Leggings." Just like the toothpaste and the hand warmers, every time we snuggled into those leggings, we were reminded how much we were loved.

With performing comes clothes. The right outfit can make or break the spirit of a teenage girl when she's gearing up for a performance. Whenever she performs, I think we spend as much time picking out just the right outfit as she does actually preparing for the performance. When she was offered the opportunity to do her own cabaret show, the first thing out of her mouth was "I have to get an amazing dress, Mama." With the best smile I could muster in that moment, all I could say was "oh, we will find the perfect dress." Great. I was living in arguably one of the most expensive cities in the world and she needed an "amazing" dress. Amazing just wasn't in my budget. Pretty was in my budget. Her own cabaret show at eighteen wasn't in our plan, either, but it was happening. I told her we would start shopping early so we could save up to get that perfect dress. No matter what I had to do, I was determined to find it. Thus enters another treasured blessing along this journey.

We met Rob and Stephanie White many years before through a mutual friend in a business relationship. We were never really close but knew each other well enough. #babybird had spent some time with Rob and his daughter and had some great memories, but that's kind of where it ended. We had lived here about a year, I guess, when I received a Facebook message from Rob. It was odd at first because we had never really been close friends. What followed in that message left me speechless. It was one of the kindest notes I have ever read. He told me how proud he was of her, but more importantly of me. He said that I was a great example of a parent putting their child's life above their own. It was truly a touching message that I will never forget. For many months after receiving it, I would re-read it from time to time when I was feeling down and beaten up by this city. From there, we began to converse a little more often, just keeping them in the know about her accomplishments and life in the big city. They made a visit the following summer and we spent time just hanging around and getting to know one another again. Since that first message, I couldn't possibly count the number of times Rob has told me how proud he is of us. Each time, it's like a little shot in the arm that just propels us forward.

When they got word of the cabaret, they were so excited and began to plan their trip. They wanted to be part of this first big milestone in her career and we were so happy to have them. But that wasn't where the love stopped. I received a PayPal notification one day and it was from Rob. I was extremely puzzled when the email popped across my phone. I didn't think Rob owed me any money and I was pretty sure I didn't owe him anything either.

But it wasn't for a debt. It was for a dress.

#babybird's cabaret debut dress to be exact. He said to me on the phone later, "we want her to buy the dress of her dreams with her not having to worry about the price tag." Oddly enough, that was my dream, too. I wanted this first show to be spectacular in every way. She had worked so hard and sacrificed so much I just wanted her to have a beautiful new gown in which to make her debut.

I could never have afforded the dress that her heart desired. I mean I could have stretched and skipped a few grocery visits but starvation for a dress just didn't seem to be a wise parenting move to me. I had already made a number of decisions that some people in our lives considered questionable, at best. I figured with this one, it might be best not to press my luck. It was a priceless gift. She could shop without worry if it fit into the budget. We found the perfect dress the first time out shopping. It literally fit like it was made to be worn by her. She pulled it out more times than I can count over the months leading up to her show. She said she needed to "practice in it," and that "it made her transform into performer mode." Oddly enough, she was right. Every time she put it on, it transformed her, right there in the middle of my kitchen.

Rob and Stephanie have kids and grandkids of their own, but they chose to do something remarkable for mine. As a single mom, that's a special kind of compassion that can't simply be explained. I will be eternally grateful beyond anything they could ever imagine for this precious gift. Just like the toothpaste, and the hand warmers and the leggings, it was a sign of love and support. It wasn't the price tag that made it priceless to us. It was the intent behind it.

They believed in her.

They believed in us.

And, that's what made it priceless.

When you think about teachers, rarely do you think about making friends for life. That is, unless you are The Peterson Girls. #babybird has fallen in love with nearly every teacher she has ever had. In middle school, she developed a particularly special relationship with her teachers at Horace Mann Middle School. They were a wonderfully supportive group of ladies who poured into her as a student long before we ever even entertained the thought of moving. They range from a science teacher she never actually had to another science teacher who was a junior high classmate of mine, to an English teacher (now a vice principal) who started going to our church right about the time we moved.

The middle school years were abnormally hard on #babybird because her Nana was her sickest during those years. My sweet girl spent many afternoons at her Nana's house helping her clean up, doing her laundry, and even cooking for her when she wasn't feeling up to it.

My girl has never been one to hold anything in. If she has feelings, she tells you. If she went somewhere fun, she tells you. She is not afraid to lay it out there without any worry about how it might be construed. I don't have to tell you that she got this honestly. I fully believe that we all need a therapist from time to time in our lives to help us process difficult things. For us, that was our village. Whether they wanted to be or not, they were the people we turned to when we needed to talk. And, we pretty much always need to talk about something.

Her teachers all knew that her Nana was sick. They also knew that she was providing a lot of care to her while I worked. And they knew the toll that could take on our little family. They asked her nearly every day, "How's your Nana today? Is your Mama doing ok? Is there anything you girls need?" Just those few words forged relationships that nearly held her together the last few years before Nana left us.

One of the most influential of these wonderful humans was her 6th grade English teacher and her husband, Steve and Joanne Gregory. They have a grown son and a grandson, but they somehow found room in their hearts for these two crazy girls. They love me as a daughter and her as a granddaughter. They never forget Christmas or birthdays and there was always room at "their inn" if we ever needed a place to stay when we came to town.

But our relationship with them wasn't just about them folding us into their lives and treating us like family; at least not so much for me. My relationship with them represented security of some sort. Another set of "parentals" that I knew I could always count on should I need anything. Like the toothpaste, it doesn't seem like a big thing. In fact, in this case it's not a thing at all. It's a feeling - a feeling of security that you simply cannot put a price tag on. It's peace when I sleep at night. It's knowing we always have a place in their home. It's knowing that with a simple phone call these people, who have no biological relationship to us, would drop everything to rescue us if we needed it. It's a feeling of support and love that has remained a foundational part of our journey.

One of the things we love about them is their love of food! Steve is one heck of a cook and you can tell when he is in the kitchen, he is putting a little love in every move he makes. If there was a Love Language called "Cooking" that would be Steve. It is always a sure bet that our visits with them will include something yummy. At our holiday lunch with the whole gang two things are always on the menu: sausage balls for me and a cookies and cream ice cream shake for #babybird. (As alike as #babybird and I are, in this way we are different. I want salt, she wants sweet.) Anyway, it's always a feast and a wonderful time to catch everyone up on all the happenings in the big city.

Our love for Steve and Joanne is one of those things that I will never be able to quantify. Like the toothpaste, our relationship with them is an almost daily expression of love that we will carry with us forever. They don't necessarily send us toothpaste, but in other ways, they take a little piece of the emotional burden of living in this big city off my shoulders.

But it wasn't just WV reaching out to show us love. God made sure to start expanding our tribe here in NYC. People ask me all the time, "what is the hardest part about living in the city? The subway? (honestly, with my FB rants this would be a logical conclusion for anyone) How expensive everything is? Your microscopic apartment?" In truth, those things are hard. And they did take some adjusting. But the single hardest part? Relationships. Home is always home. And there will always be people there that we keep in touch with and feel encouraged by. But doing life next to people, that's a necessity.

God is very clear that we were made for relationships and he wasn't just talking about marriage. He was talking about all relationships, including friendships. For the first two years of our adventure, we made some connections. But neither of us really felt like we were forging deep relationships that we needed to become the fabric of our lives. Relationships take time to grow and become that fabric, but we had met very few people along our journey that were being woven into our tribe.

Let me be clear, we were (are) well loved! You are probably tired of hearing it, but I am going to keep saying it as a reminder to all those people that have stayed the course with us through the best and worst of times along this crazy journey. I am abundantly thankful for those who stayed the course for "my" worst of times. Single moms don't always make rational decisions where their hearts are concerned. Trust me, I have the life evidence to prove it.

During #babybird's sophomore year of high school (about 2 years into this adventure), I began to get more involved. If you know me, I don't dip my toe into anything. I dive in head first with everything I have and worry about what to do next when I come up for my first breath. I truly live by the motto, you can do anything you put your mind to - well, almost anything that is. It was in this "diving in" that I met my friend Nicole Wright. She had a daughter who was a junior in the dance program. For some cosmic reason we immediately hit it off. I think our no-nonsense approach to raising kids and pushing through life was a connection for us.

The school PTA had been a disaster for several years. It had all but exploded under the leadership of an interesting group of parents. Fresh faced and ready to be "the hands-on parent" led me to the post of co-chair of the annual school gala. Up to this point I had planned a LOT of stuff. Parties, weddings, baby showers, corporate events - but I had never planned a school gala with an auction. Long story short, as a result of my endeavor into the unknown, Nicole and I became friends. Not the kind of friends that you talk to every single day. Sometimes not even in a month or two. But when we ran into each other, the connection was there, and it was comforting.

Nicole showed up for that gala ready to work! She jumped right in and helped make that evening a smashing success. We were kindred in the way we embraced good, hard work. That year, her daughter graduated. We didn't talk as often after school ended, so I figured the chances of us actually keeping in contact were slim, but I was choosing to be grateful for the encounters we did have and not sad for what I thought would be a short lived friendship. I firmly believe people are brought into our world when we need them most. I know it sounds cliché, but some stay for a lifetime, others for just a season. I was okay if Nicole was just here for a season.

Shortly after graduation she reached out and invited me for what we now call "play dates." It took us a little finagling to get our schedules to work (which oddly enough still seems to be our biggest challenge even though all our kids are out of school), but we finally met and had one of the most meaningful conversations I had experienced since moving to NYC. It was truly amazing.

But it wasn't that one coffee that landed her in this book in the chapter about the little things that people did to support us. What landed her here was (is) her relentless pursuit of my friendship. Again, nothing tangible like toothpaste, or vintage dresses, or things to keep us warm. She committed time to growing our friendship and sharing through life's challenges. She truly wanted to see me. She wanted to carve out time from her busy schedule to hang out with me. (did I mention she is a mom of three with a husband, a full-time job, and a full-time school schedule?) She is a New Yorker. Northerners, as we call them where we are from, have a reputation outside of this city to be cold and unfriendly. And, honestly, some are. BUT she showed me a different type of big city person. The kind of person I expected to find in WV, not here. She is one of so many people we have encountered on this journey who are just the opposite of what we were told to expect. They are warm, compassionate, encouraging, and all kinds of other awesomely positive adjectives that you could imagine. All amazing. (I hope this dispels the misunderstanding that NY'ers are cold and uncaring - because most of them are just the opposite).

I have been a single mom for nearly all of #babybird's life. With the exception of one boyfriend, it's always just been me. Everyone around me was married. Or divorced and remarried. No matter how intentional the invitations were to spend time with their families, I could never shake the feeling of "let's love on the single mom who doesn't have anyone, so she feels loved." Let me make this clear - I have been loved well. All around. And my circle never set out to make me or any other of their single friends feel that way. But no matter how sincere their love was, there are always moments when we single moms (and dads) feel our singleness. Even with well-meaning friends who truly love you and want you around, it's sometimes hard to not feel the "one of these doesn't look like the other" emotions that come from a wonderful Thanksgiving dinner with a large, loving family.

Nicole wanted to be with me because she cherished our friendship. She saw me, not my singleness. She connected with the friend side of me which had little to do with being a wife or a mother. She wasn't my friend because our girls were friends. #babybird and her daughter ran in separate circles mostly because they were not the same age and in different majors. We were two strong women with very different lifestyles. But she understood NYC and the loneliness that could overtake normal thoughts of fitting in. She knew how hard it was to make meaningful friendships, and she chose to befriend a single mom from somewhere nowhere near NYC. That, my friends, is compassion and love at its very best.

I am happy to report that our play dates have continued. We are two strong women from very different lifestyles doing life as two friends should - together. It's surely not a tube of toothpaste, or a beautiful dress. But that doesn't make it any less important. As a matter of fact, it's a small thing in her life that has given me the strength to stand back up when NYC tried to keep me down.

When you add up all these "little" things it becomes something big. An unseen layer of support and love that we never knew we needed until we had it. As I began to really focus on writing this book, I couldn't stop thinking about all the million little things that held us together. I could write three more books and tell story after story of the many people who have blessed us with little things that have made our lives easier, and encouragement that seems to come just when we need it most.

It's humbling to say the least.

The world we live in today can sometimes be a scary place. Love has been replaced with hate. Neighbors are turning on each other because they disagree about one thing or another. Families are being torn apart by petty differences. My heart physically aches when I hear of the hurt that people experience unnecessarily.

But there is also kindness. All of these little things are proof positive of that. I like to think of them as little rain drops from Heaven. It's God's way of reminding us there is good in this world, and it's up to us to spread it widely. We need to be better to each other. We need to turn those little drops into bucketfuls and then waterfalls, until kindness spreads farther than our eyes can see.

I promise you this, all those tiny drops that people so generously let fall into our buckets are the very things that have kept this ship afloat.

CHAPTER EIGHT

Train Logic

Train Logic = Life Logic

Once I decided to turn my journals into a book for public consumption, I began to look back over my entries and social media posts, to pick out things that seemed book worthy or things I thought people might find inspiring or funny. As I read through some of these, my little mind began to draw parallels between the nonsense of our train experiences traveling from one corner of this city to the other, to life lessons that could apply no matter where we lived.

If you are a native NY'er, you are probably going to think this chapter is silly. I get it, but this chapter isn't for you. It's for all of those outside of this big city who are curious about how we have adjusted after basically trading in our cute little car named Henrietta, with her pretty eyelashes, for a not so cute, never on time, dirty subway.

Oddly enough, a decent amount of this book was written while riding on, stuck on or waiting on the dumb train. I am actually somewhat surprised that the phrases "there is a train ahead of

us, train traffic, a sick passenger, or being held by the station"
didn't accidentally creep their way into nearly every chapter of this
book in some way or another. Heaven knows those statements are
burned into my mind after five years of subway riding.

People always ask, "What's it like riding the subway
everywhere?" My standard answer is, "it's not awful, well,
sometimes it's awful, actually it's pretty much always awful, and
makes me question humanity and truly fear for our future." I
know that sounds dramatic, but if you would see what we see on
a daily basis, I assure you, you would feel the same. My friend,
Kristy Cates-Frankfort, even wrote a song and filmed a video
called *Kristy's Lament: Another Day on the Awful MTA* about her
train adventures. Hop on over to YouTube when you have a
moment and check it out. It's pretty hysterical, and if you aren't
a NY'er, you should know - every single bit of that actually
happens! And sometimes all of it in one single ride!

By now you can probably guess the MTA and I are not generally
friends. Anyone who follows me on social media sees my almost
daily rants about their general lack of professionalism and care
for the people who rely on the subway system to get around this
city. It's not like they are building an entire new infrastructure!
As you can tell by my tone, it truly is a love-hate relationship I
have with the MTA. Mostly hate. I know, you are truly shocked at
my hostility.

I remember the first time I was on a train that suddenly "went
express" without notice. For non-NY'ers that means your train
just decided to skip a bunch of stops. Then, before I knew it, we
were going local again but skipping random stops. I remember
thinking to myself, "does this dumb train even know where it's
going?" By the time they changed lines, skipped a few stops and
went express, I wasn't sure I knew where I was going.

We rely heavily on the Google Maps and CityMapper apps on
our phone and the digital signs that are in most stations that
show the estimated time of arrival for trains coming into the
station. I say estimated because they usually aren't right. We
always check both apps and the sign and the trains come
somewhere in the middle of those three times. None of them are
ever the same - or right. Go figure.

Case in point, one of our most ridiculous train adventures to
date happened on what started as a normal Sunday morning. It
was gloomy and raining on and off as we headed out to church.
We get to our station and the electronic sign says the next R train
is 19 minutes away. But the next E train is only 6 minutes away.

This is perfect, because the E train actually gets us much closer than the R anyway and it's coming first. Both apps were estimating around the same time, so we felt confident in assuming that we were going to be on the train we wanted and would make it to church on time. That's what we get for making assumptions. We end up waiting 21 minutes and neither the E or the R showed up. Instead, an F train showed up. The problem is, the F train gets us nowhere near as close as the R or the E. On a beautiful spring morning this wouldn't be too much of an issue, but on a rainy morning this was torture. And who really wants to walk on a cold rainy morning if you don't have to?

The digital sign now said 26 minutes for the R and 18 minutes for the E. I can only assume the sign had been infiltrated with a stream of rainwater that came down through the cracks in the ceiling big enough for small children to fit through during this rainstorm. At this point we had zero clue what train was coming and when. Having played this game before, we decide getting the F was our best chance of getting close enough to church so that we could be remotely on time.

As we pull out of the station, the conductor announces the F train is running on the E line between Jamaica Avenue and Manhattan. Great news! Remember, the E is closer to church anyway. We are happy about the sudden route change, but the people next to us are clearly peeved because they don't want to be on the E line. As usual, the conductor waited until after the doors were closed and the train had begun to pull out of the station before he made the announcement, thus trapping these poor people on a train they didn't want to be on. I have learned to spot tourists by their eyes. I could tell that these people were visiting our fair city and our subway system was just smacking them around that morning.

Two stops later, the conductor announces that this F train - remember it was running on the E line into Manhattan - has changed its mind and is now back on the F line, which pretty much messes us up again (and half the other people on the train by the sounds of their grunts as the words came over the loudspeaker). As we begin to recalculate our journey, the conductor comes back on and tells passengers they can get off at 53rd Street and wait for the next E train which WILL be making local stops. Exercising extreme trust, we get off that train and wait for the next Brooklyn bound E train to arrive - which doesn't come for 10 minutes. This was the same train that the conductor said was "right behind this train." I don't know what his definition of "right behind" was, but 10 minutes is not right behind in my book. Even better, after it finally arrives, and we load into it - clearly over packed - it goes past just one station, and literally stops and sits still for 20 minutes. Not once in that 20 minutes did that conductor even so much as breathe over that loudspeaker, much less tell us what was happening.

At this point, two seemingly quiet men pull out their guitars and begin to try to walk through the overly crowded train to serenade us all with their mirachi selections at 8:45am on that fine Sunday morning. If they thought they had a captive audience that would reward their music, they were sadly mistaken. What they had was a sweat box full of angry people ready to tear into one another with no warning.

We have now been in route for 50 minutes, traded trains twice, and are 30 minutes late for church. It's like something breaks in my mind and I am now a raging lunatic - on my way to church, mind you. Clearly the place I needed to be to repent of all the horrible things my mind conjured up to do to this train conductor and the woman behind me who kept flinging her oversized purse into my back. I swear she dug into that thing at least a dozen times for heaven knows what in the 20 minutes we were stuck. If he didn't get this train moving soon, I was 100% certain I was going to find out how I looked in an orange jumpsuit. Do you think these conductors realized they were messing with the mental state of a woman in menopause who could literally snap at any moment?

We eventually made it, but walked farther than we wanted and ended up soaked. But this story (and the million other ones shared daily by subway riders) begs the question, "Why have a map if the subway can at any moment go somewhere totally different?"

Up until this moment, you have heard my belly aching, but I have to share that through all the challenges of our transportation woes, we have learned many life lessons. So, I am going to climb back up on my soapbox and share some of them.

I can't tell you how many times we have literally had a train door close in our faces. As if the train Gods were saying, "See what happens when you hit that snooze button one extra time?" I get it. It was all about trying to avoid touching your warm feet onto the cold floor that sent a chill through your entire body, because you knew that was an indication of just how cold it was going to be outside for your morning walk to the train. The problem is that extra ten minutes just bumped you from standing comfortably on the rush hour train, to being a human sardine in this sweatbox of a train car that basically had the heat turned up so high, someone was going to faint and cause the entire line to run on extensive delays while they waited on the EMTs to come help. I wish I were joking, but this is the daily life of most of us who ride the subway to work.

Hear this - time is precious. We spend so much time commuting. For us it's a train. For you it might be a car, or a boat or a plane. Whichever way you get around, use it wisely. Don't waste it. Listen to a podcast instead of the radio. Carry this into your homes. Read a book instead of watching TV. Sit in a room with your family and just talk. You can't get back those lost moments.

Our lesson in the ridiculousness of subway riding has been to use that time to do something productive. Read a book. Heck, write a book! Learn music. Pray. Knit. Those are moments where we can be captive to something our hearts desire. It's easy to let those moments get sucked into the abyss. It's also easy to use those moments to feed our soul. Choose wisely.

#babybird and I have had many conversations over the last five years about being careful: careful when riding the train; careful when making friends; careful when in a large crowd of people we don't know; careful when we share intimate parts of our story with strangers. It's a reality of life. We all have to be careful and keep our hearts protected. NYC has taught us how to live life with our eyes wide open and that was never truer than when we learned to be careful of entering empty train cars.

I remember the first time this happened like it was yesterday. We were standing on the platform waiting on the train. As it zooms past, we noticed that all the cars were packed, and our hopes of a seat were slipping through our fingers like sand through the hourglass in the opening credits of the old soap opera, *Days of our Lives*. All of a sudden there it is - a completely EMPTY train car in the middle of rush hour with a ton of seats AND it stopped RIGHT IN FRONT OF US! Praise the Lord. Without a moment's thought, we rushed into the train and beelined for two seats together. It took five seconds and that first breath for us to realize we had just made a huge mistake. This train car was empty for a reason and that reason was strewn all over the seats across from us. Someone's lunch had clearly not settled well, and they had left it all splattered all over this train car. Yes, vomit. An entire bench of the foulest smelling, most disgusting looking regurgitated food I had ever seen.

I work in medicine. I have seen a lot of gross things in my career. But this. Never. Never had I ever seen anything so repulsive in my life. And the smell. OMGosh! How in the world every car on that train didn't smell remains an absolute mystery to me. But here we are. The doors have closed, and we are trapped. In that moment, there were no other prayers that ranked higher for us than getting out of that train car. I wish I could say we only fell for that once, but I can't. There were a few other times. Not quite as disgusting as that one, but nonetheless we were kicking ourselves the moment the doors closed and we found ourselves trapped.

In life, you have to pay attention to what is around you, be it people, or places or scents. (both good and bad) You have to be aware. We don't live in a Pollyanna world anymore where we can skip down dirt roads until dark whistling a happy tune and know that Mama and Daddy will be waiting on the porch to scoop us into the bath and off to bed, so we could rise and play another day.

News flash! Not everyone or everything around you is going to be good for you. I know, that stings a little. Just because we want it, doesn't mean it's good for us. Just like looking into that train car that day, what was on the other side was NOT good for us. We had our blinders on and didn't stop to take two seconds to see the whole picture - just what we wanted to see. A couple of empty seats.

I would love to tell you that every person we have met was instantly connected to us and enriched every second of the time we spent with them. But if I said that, it wouldn't be the truth. I made a vow when I decided to write this book that I would be 100% honest, all the way through. The honest truth is we have met people that weren't good for either one of us.

Listen, we love people. No matter who you are, what race or religion you are, where you live, whom you live with or what job you have. We. Love. You. Of all the earthly gifts God has given us, I am most grateful for the gift of love. The ability to see past differences and embrace humans for what they bring to our lives. I believe in the depth of my soul if Jesus himself were walking the earth today, this is exactly how he would love.

But we have met some people that just weren't good for us and had to say some hard goodbyes and "we wish you wells" along this journey. I wish everyone had good intentions and wanted what is best for those around them, but that's not true either. I am certain there will be more hard encounters to come, because that's just part of life. Just remember, always keep your eyes open, and be careful not to run into an empty train car - for you never know what's waiting on the other side.

There are two times that I really dread riding the subway. Oddly enough, both situations have taught me one of the most important life lessons I could ever pass on to my #babybird - when to show grace. When to look the other way and make no assumptions. When to back off and let people have a not so great moment without fear of judgement.

For example, you just can't avoid being on a train squished together with strangers when you take the subway to and from work. I have become pretty masterful at timing my morning commute to avoid those windows in time where I know it's going to feel like I am packed into a can of sardines.

But every now and then, I get sandwiched in so tight I don't need to hold a pole, I just lean into whomever is surrounding me and we kind of hold each other up. But there are moments when I get irritated. Not because we are packed in, because we all know that happens. I get mad when someone brings more stuff along than what I find is an acceptable amount on a rush hour train. You know, the one lady who has her purse, briefcase, suitcase and three shopping bags. She takes up more room that ten people on the train and she is giving anyone who looks her way the stink eye.

One day it occurred to me as I glanced down into someone's bag and realized that maybe they weren't just being an obnoxious rider bringing all their stuff along knowing they were going to torture all the other riders. This woman appeared to have everything she owned with her. I saw a blender, shoe polish, wash cloths and a cheese grater stuffed into this bag that was bursting open. Her purse had make-up overflowing and a briefcase was filled with books.

I had nothing else to do, so I began to imagine what her story looked like. Was she dramatically moving out of her parent's home on a crusade to prove to the world that she was an independent woman? Or had she been kicked out because her mother suddenly had a new boyfriend and no time for her young adult daughter? Had she had a fight with her own boyfriend, frantically packed all she could and headed to her girlfriend's house, hoping that when he came home and saw the blender and the cheese grater gone, that he would come searching for her and beg her to come back? Or did she have only five minutes while he was in the shower to grab as much as she could and bolt so that he wouldn't raise a hand to her yet again?

I don't know why she had all that stuff. It wasn't my business. But my first instinct was to judge her. I was angry that she was filling up so much space that I had to stand way too close to the man who had literally bathed in cheap cologne and had sticky fingers that somehow kept finding my derriere every time the train hit a bump. At that moment, what she needed was my grace and a little understanding, not my judgment. I will never know why she carted what looked like everything she owned onto that train car that morning, but I do know that when those situations have creeped up again along our journey, instead of being mad, I now choose to show grace. Maybe she was just being a jerk, but maybe she wasn't. I will never know - but what I will always know is that I gave grace, and that's enough.

The same could be true for my second least favorite time on the train. When someone smells. Yes, smells. You get on the train and find that someone has their hand or their scarf covering their face trying not to breathe in whatever unpleasant smell is nearby. I do it. I'm not going to lie. And for the first moment or two, I am usually pretty ticked off, looking for a way to steer clear of the offender. Then it happens. I make eye contact and I realize who it is. You can see deep into their soul of embarrassment. They look away quickly, knowing what you must be thinking of them.

What if this poor person's water wasn't working that morning? Or maybe, they don't even HAVE water where they live. Who am I to pass judgment on this unsuspecting human that may have zero control over how they smell at that moment. Then I stop, close my eyes, and remember - grace. The more grace we give out, the more grace-filled this world becomes. And the more grace-filled this world becomes, the less we have to worry about things like "being careful before getting onto an empty train car."

But amidst all the mushy life lessons, not all train rides have been filled with situations that pull at our heartstrings. One of these days, I am going to knock the lights out of the pole dancers. Yes, non-NY'ers, I said pole dancers. Listen, I support the arts. I love to see creative people BE creative and do what they love, especially if it involves music. But for the love of all things Holy, please stop using the subway pole as your "dance pole." You look like a fool and no one needs to have their fingers smashed under your feet while you attempt to show the world that you can spin your body around a pole. Just don't. (ask #babybird about her encounter with a pole dancer if you want a comical story!)

The only thing worse than a pole dancer is a pole hugger. These are the people who think that the entire pole belongs to them and they wrap their arms around it and cuddle it like you would a body pillow, not leaving even a centimeter open so another rider could use it to help balance them on their ride. They lean their entire body against the pole so they can be on their phone while they ride without worry of falling because they use the pole to balance themselves.

I don't care if you are a pole hugger or a pole leaner. I AM going to push my hand in there to hold the pole. I don't care how much you huff and puff at me or shoot me a nasty look. You WILL share this pole with me, and if you don't like it you can either find yourself a seat or get off and find another train car. Because my $2.75 is just as valuable as yours, and part of that pole belongs to me as much as it does to you.

Beyond the pole huggers/leaners, you have the seat stealers. These are the people who don't want strangers sitting next to them so they pile up their "stuff" in the seat so no one can sit there. I probably don't need to tell you that I am THAT PERSON who walks over and says, "excuse me, can you please move your bag so I can sit?" Then stand with eyes locked until they do.

And you gotta watch out for the little old ladies who are in shape. They will mow you down to get to that one open seat. I am not kidding, they will literally knock you over. These women are in far better shape than I could ever hope to be in, and they are determined to get themselves to that seat and they could care less who they trip or knock over in the process. If you even remotely look like you are getting up, you will be swarmed by every one of them in that car just waiting to dive into it when you stand up. Heck, they won't think twice about taking EACH OTHER out to get that seat, either.

Riding the train has become a game for #babybird and I these last few years. We are braver now than when we first arrived and our tolerance for stupidity is significantly lower than on November 9, 2014, when we unloaded that rental truck and set down roots. We love to see how uncomfortable we can make people who are being total jerks on the train. I know, judge if you will, but we aren't asking anyone to do anything that isn't on the human decency list that we should all be living by.

I will leave you with one tender moment, probably my MOST tender subway moment ever. I had been riding the N train (above ground at the 30th Street Station) for about three months. I knew if I got on the very end of the train it would put me out at the end of the platform that would take me to the street corner that allowed for the shortest outside walk to my office. It was winter, and if I could cut two blocks off my walk when it was freezing, that's what I was going to do. I am a creature of habit, so I left home at the same time every day and usually rode the train with the same people. I also saw the same conductor at least three days a week. I always said "good morning" to him. In the beginning, he just grumbled under his breath irritated that I was being so nice, I assume. Eventually, he would smile and finally we got to the "good morning" phase. I always had my coffee with me - literally the only way that I made it through the first hour of my morning most days - and he eventually made jokes about my mugs. They were pink and colorful. Always. One morning, as I was walking down the platform to go in "my door" I see him lean out of his window. He has a cup of coffee in his hand and he is reaching it towards me. He very quietly handed it to me and said, "thank you for always being kind. I hope you have a great day." He closed his window, I stepped onto the train and off we went. It was a quiet, but beautiful exchange I will never forget.

Eventually, I started riding another train and I never saw him again. But I will never forget his face. He had kind eyes, and I knew he had been eaten up by the same subway nonsense that we all deal with on a daily basis. I hope that for those nine months that my simple "good morning" gave him a small amount of joy to carry throughout his day. His cup of coffee sure did that for me.

I could write multiple novels about our train adventures. And you would laugh at every single story. While most of the time the train tests our patience and our ability to hold our tempers and our tongues, neither one of us would change a single moment of fun we have had becoming subway commuters over the last five years. Well, we probably could have lived without that empty train car throw up incident, but whatever...

CHAPTER NINE

The Right People
The Right Place
The Right Time

That's the name of this game

No one will ever convince me that anyone we have met on this journey was by mere coincidence. I will go to my grave believing that every single person was hand-picked by God and dropped into our lives at pivotal points to help this journey unfold the way that it has. When I say we have favor, friends, I mean it. Bucketfuls and bucketfuls of favor. Can I get an Amen?!

One of our first lessons about this business was that talent isn't enough. It's also about timing and people. And, being easy to work with and coachable. But people really are what hold a career together in this business. Some people teach. Some people mentor. Some people are connectors. Some people cast shows. Some people represent talent. Some people manage talent. MANY people buy tickets to watch shows. No matter how you look at it, people are at the core of everything that makes this business work.

When I began to think about all the people we have met that changed the course of our journey, all I could see in my head was a map. I know calling it a map is a funny way to pull this together, but it's the only word that truly describes what it looks like when you trace back to where all these people became part of our story. It's like a giant connect the dots sheet.

The day we met Kim Myers started like any other normal December morning. I like to call her our very first connector. One of the most influential connections she made for us, was meeting Roger DelPozo from The New York Film Academy (NYFA). Offering #babybird that infamous scholarship to NYFA's summer camp was just one of the amazing ways Roger helped us make the jump. He recommended books and met us to check in on the progress of our move on one of our house hunting tours. I will never forget how encouraging he was. And let me tell you, I am certain my endless list of dumb questions gave him good reason to put me in the "crazy mom" column.

During our first conversation with him at The ARTS he said, "she's really good. She just needs a little training so she can learn to use her mix." I remember looking at #babybird because I didn't have a clue what her "mix" even was. (Thankfully, she did. Thank you, Ms. Noel and Mr. Bryan.) He was so encouraging and real. It was one of the first moments where I think the realization that she might just have a future in this business really hit me.

He talked to me a few times over the phone after we left ARTS, and when we finally pulled the trigger and set a plan in motion, Roger told me to reach out once we were settled, because he had a voice teacher that he thought would be a great match for #babybird.

I spoke with Roger while writing this book and he said to me, "when I initially saw and heard #babybird perform, it was evident that she had incredible natural ability as well as a drive and maturity way beyond her years." As I read these words, my heart swells just a little bit. It was truly in the plan for Roger to be in that place at that moment, to see #babybird take her first flight.

True to his word, Roger introduced us to our beloved first voice teacher here in NYC, Kristy Cates. We met Kristy first over the phone. We had lived here all of about a month. She was on maternity leave with her own brand-new bundle of joy, Grace Opal. She was kind, knowledgeable and seemed genuinely excited to meet us. There was one moment during our conversation that I will never forget. She shared that she had watched some of #babybird's YouTube videos. "When I watched some of her videos online, I saw my younger self in her." That's pretty much all we needed to hear. We both had a feeling in our gut that she was the right teacher for this season of her journey, so we scheduled a lesson and #babybird began counting the days.

I will never forget that first lesson. It was so much more than I could have ever imagined. After we had all said "hello" and had our moment of being starstruck (Kristy was in the original cast of *Wicked* and to #babybird she was like royalty), I retreated to the hallway to let them get down to business. It was so hard to leave that room. I wanted so much to stay, but I knew my place was in the hallway. She needed her time to establish a relationship with who we hoped would be her voice teacher.

That first lesson was pure magic. It had been so long since I had seen #babybird so exhilarated and ready to do the hard work that would come with this life she craved. Kristy spoke a language that #babybird understood. She was making sounds I had never heard before.

Kristy was also responsible for our first backstage tour of a real Broadway show. In the early days everything about this place made #babybird explode with excitement, but nothing will ever match the excitement of seeing Kristy on that stage. THEN, to have her be the one to take us on a tour of what happens behind the curtain was like icing on the big cake of life.

Over the last five years #babybird has had countless lessons with Kristy. We have seen her shine on stage in two Broadway shows, and we have forged a beautiful relationship outside of the rehearsal room with her sweet family. We love our Gracie beyond words and I hope to always be her "Aunt Feffie."

After about three lessons, Kristy suggested #babybird look into a program called The Broadway Workshop, run by Marc Tuminelli. Kristy had known Marc for a long time and thought it would be a good place for #babybird to get her feet wet. It just so happened Marc was casting for his next Mainstage Production, *Bring It On*, the following week. Without hesitation #babybird was all in.

If you know #babybird then you already know the irony of her playing a cheerleader. We had seen the national tour of *Bring It*

On the summer before we moved. The show was great, but there was an entire evening of jokes about this being one show that she could never do because cheerleader material she was not. Obviously, God had a sense of humor. A big one. She was cast as a cheerleader.

This was by far the VERY BEST introduction to the youth theater scene in NYC that we could have ever asked for. Talented kids and a director that knew how to make the hard work fun, resulting in a truly amazing production. She bounced home each and every weekend with an excitement I had yet to see in her. The best part of her experience was that Marc wasn't just providing an opportunity for her to be in a show with a bunch of talented kids. He was teaching her, and the rest of the cast, the art of performing and she was soaking in every single second of those rehearsals.

Marc stacked his team with seasoned Broadway performers and treated the cast as if they were working on a professional show. He had high expectations of these kids and he knew how to bring out the best in them. #babybird would go on to do two more shows with him before graduating high school. Every single show was exceptional. If you ask her, she will tell you, those shows were not only a lot of fun, but they were also a safe place where she could let her guard down and be accepted for who she was. And that made my mom heart rest easy.

Bring It On definitely found its way into our favorites playlist, right alongside another show that was a Broadway smash, *Mamma Mia*. We actually saw *Mamma Mia* four times. It would be the first of several shows that we loved so much we wanted to take every person who visited to see it.

The first time we saw it was in September 2014. The decision had been made to move to NYC and we were on a house hunting trip. This is the show that taught us what "stage dooring" actually meant. You race out at the end of the shows to the back doors of the theater. After the bows of course. You never leave before the bows are over, people! You stand behind these metal barricades and wait for the performers to come out and sign your *Playbill*, say "hello," and take selfies. She loved this part almost as much as watching the show. These people represented everything she wanted to be. They were the biggest stars in the world in her eyes (and, still are).

We have met many amazing performers over the years, but one will always stand out above the rest. Lauren "Coco" Cohn played Rosie, one of the two best friends of Donna, Sophie's mother, in *Mamma Mia*. Hilarious and brilliant. The two best words I can think of to describe her performance. Which also happens to describe her personality, too.

For #babybird the magic really happened at the stage door. Coco was kind, spunky and very generous with her time. Without even realizing it, #babybird basically vomited her life story in thirty seconds, ending with, "I am moving here in three weeks and someday I am going to be on Broadway, too." Now, she would have had every right to sign that Playbill with a smile and scoot on down to the next person. But she didn't. She was truly interested and wanted to know more. It was one of those moments that you will just never forget. (As I type this, I have a tear running down my face.)

Fast-forward a few months and I see a post on Facebook that she was directing a kids cabaret. When I shared it with #babybird, she squealed with excitement and we knew she had to audition. She walked out of that audition grinning from ear to ear. Coco had remembered their stage door meeting and #babybird was over the moon. A real Broadway star had recognized this little girl from Charleston, WV. Thankfully, #babybird was cast in that cabaret and had the opportunity to work one-on-one with Coco. She went on to do several more kids cabaret shows with Coco, each one better than the last, and now sometimes she even steps in as her stage manager!

Fast forward again - three years this time - and we were in the thick of producing #babybird's first solo cabaret and I was feeling a little overwhelmed. When I say producing, that's my VERY LOOSE interpretation of trying to hold it all together and not having a single clue what I was doing. Without one single second of hesitation #babybird said, "Let's call Coco. She gets me. Maybe she can help!" We reached out and thankfully she agreed to meet with us and just talk over the big picture. I was just hoping she would have some ideas to help me pull this together. And boy did she have ideas! Out the wazoo, people. All this time I have talked about how much #babybird learned, but in this season of that cabaret, I believe I learned as much as she did, and uncovered something I love to do - write and create!

Long story short, Coco joined #teambabybird and together we created a remarkable debut show that really represented the very best of #babybird. She was right. Coco gets her. She sees her passion and understands her dreams. I am happy to share that she has become not just a director/teacher for us, she has also become a treasured friend to both of us. There is no question about the important role she continues to play in fostering

#babybird's love for theater and performing.

Speaking of that first cabaret show, my, oh my. Talk about the right people at the right time, this connection was truly divine. We met KT Sullivan, Artistic Director, Mabel Mercer Foundation, when #babybird competed in The 1st Annual Mabel's Babies competition. It was a cabaret competition for high school kids, that was intended to help keep the music of the Great American Songbook alive. If you are not a theater person, music from the Great American Songbook is also sometimes referred to as Golden Age of musical theater. Songs from this era have been recorded by some of history's most legendary singers including Judy Garland, Rosemary Clooney, Frank Sinatra, Ethel Merman, Bing Crosby, and many more. #babybird's love of this music, and MGM movie musicals, came directly from watching and falling in love with Judy Garland in her younger years. Having the opportunity to participate in this competition was like a dream come true for her.

Each contestant had the opportunity to work with KT, and her amazing music director, Jon Weber, to rehearse their selection for the competition. If you follow our story, then you already know #babybird walked away with 2nd place, which came with a nice little cash prize. It was such a fun day for both of us. But that wasn't all that came out of that competition. It also connected us to KT. She truly is a champion for young performers and #babybird loved her instantly. They bonded over their love of shoes and Judy Garland. What unfolded from this connection was so unexpected. KT offered to give #babybird one of the nights she had reserved at The Laurie Beechman Theater to stage her first solo cabaret show. Wait? What? Her own show? Could she even hold an entire show on her own?

During the months that followed, KT invited #babybird to be part of several more performing events and her little fan base began to grow. We continue to count KT and her husband, Steve, as part of our most cherished connections in this great big city. Had it not been for KT, we would never have met the great Jon Weber, who has become one of #babybird's favorite musical directors. It was almost instantaneous the way these two hit it off. Jon is a masterful music director and pianist, not to mention a really great human that we have both grown to love dearly. There is a definite connection between them that sparks a level of creativity that shines through when they work together. Jon stretches her to do things that she doesn't always think she can do, and he is truly one of her biggest cheerleaders.

After that first cabaret show, Jon (like KT) began to bring us along and give #babybird opportunities to sing time and time again. As I finish this book, they have just presented her second solo cabaret show and having the very best time you can possibly imagine collaborating, creating and making music together. And, that is priceless.

When I think back through all the people who stood behind her, it would take a four-volume set to adequately thank everyone. For example, her beloved agent, Craig Holzberg (Avalon Artist Group), met #babybird when she was only fourteen through our sweet Kristy Cates. He was doing an industry seminar just a few weeks later so we registered. These seminars are two-fold. You get to learn about the industry executive hosting the seminar, and then you get a few minutes alone with them in sort of like an audition. She got her two minutes and that was that. We had no idea where this would go, but when the call came to meet with him, we knew he was the one. From the moment we signed that first contract we have felt the whole Avalon team in her corner.

As I begin to transition the behind the scenes work that I have been keeping up with while she finished high school, I am reminded how lucky we were to have them on our team. When I thank God for bringing good, honest people into our lives, I thank him twice for Craig and his amazing team of superstars at Avalon Artist Group.

Let's not forget those who imparted wisdom on her during her four years of high school at The Professional Performing Arts School. #babybird had many teachers she loved; but three of her performing arts teachers have a solid footprint in this journey.

Jeff Statile, the director of the musical theater program, opened the door to the *Mable Babies* competition. We always say that he really set so much of the last few years in motion. He taught her first acting class during her freshman year and, from that point on, he was in her corner. He's one of those guys that you just know would do anything within his power to help if you needed it.

While Greg Parente didn't technically enter her journey formally as her teacher until her senior year, he will always be the teacher that revealed to her that she could tell a story without a song. She never wanted to do straight plays until she met him. He gave her an appreciation for Shakespeare and was one of the hardest critics she faced. He pulled no punches with her and said exactly what he thought. She will tell you that her time in his class changed her life both as a human and a performer.

As a freshman #babybird struggled. She came to this city to get to Broadway and she had no time for high school drama or kids who weren't 100% committed the day they walked into 9th grade. Arri Simon was just the person she needed to pull her back when she needed to chill out. He knew what she was capable of, and he pushed her. But my favorite part about having Mr. Simon in her life was that he never allowed her to say, "I can't." She respected him and valued the work they did together. Whenever she needed help with something, he was always the first one she called. She now works for him part time as the administrative assistant for him and his writing partner. Even after the diploma, she continues to learn from him. He, too, has become a cherished friend and continues to be part of our story!

This chapter wasn't meant to be funny or anecdotal. It was meant to say "thank you" to some of the people who stepped in and truly spent time cultivating my #songbird. There are a lot of people that have helped, way more than I could pack into this book, and we are so grateful to every single person. It's ONLY because you believed in US that we are where we are today.

CHAPTER TEN

What Is My Job Anyway?

I ain't no mama Rose!

If you don't know who Mama Rose is, let me tell you about her. In 1959, the musical *Gypsy* made its Broadway debut. It was the story of a stage mother from hell, Mama Rose, and her travels across America from theatre to theatre with her two young daughters in search of vaudeville stardom. If you are a smart mother trying to help your child navigate this business, this is the very LAST name you want to be called.

I hear it all the time. "You must be a stage mom." Ummm, no. I am not. At least not like Mama Rose. Don't get me wrong, I will ferociously protect my kid, but at the end of the day, this is her dream, not mine. And the thought of someone thinking that terrifies me.

If you have a kid deep in this business, you know the kind of mom I am talking about. Most stage moms (not all, mind you) are living vicariously through their kids' opportunities. These are the moms that coach little Susie from the back row while she is performing at the church Christmas pageant. Or the mom standing outside an audition room with her ear plastered to the door mouthing every word to little Johnny's 32-bar cut of *Consider Yourself* from *Oliver*. Listen, I get it. Our little perfect creations are just that - perfect. And it's truly baffling why everyone else in this world can't see that and cast them appropriately. (Please read that with as much sarcasm as you can muster, because that is how it is intended!)

This isn't my dream. It's hers. My dream was to see her dreams come true. Isn't that every parent's dream? I mean, we work for eighteen years to prepare them to leave and then when they do, it hits us like a ton of bricks and we act like we didn't know it was actually going to happen. Seriously, y'all, there is not one fiber of my being that was ready for her to begin the natural transition into a place where I wasn't her sole source of everything she needed to survive in this world. Plain and simple, I wasn't ready. Unfortunately, the universe really doesn't care if I am ready or not. She was getting older and more independent whether I liked it or not.

I remember that first night like it was yesterday. As I lay in bed listening to the sounds of the city, I had a moment of disbelief. (nearly twenty hours after we left WV and completely exhausted) What had we done? Did I actually sell most of what I owned and move to a city where I knew exactly ZERO people?

I sure did. I walked right up to that cliff and proceeded to step off and pray to God that I would sprout wings somewhere before we splattered on the ground of defeat. But the questions came rushing into my head faster than I could come up with solutions. Where in the world do I even begin? Do I put the dishes away or start Googling agents? Do I try to organize my teeny-tiny pantry to fit my one hundred jars of spices or look for audition opportunities? Do I scour the internet looking for just the right photographer to take just the right headshot or do I try to fit forty one years' worth of extra stuff that I just couldn't bear to part with under my full size bunk bed? I remember thinking, "I have not slept one single night in this city and I have already ruined my kids life."

That's when it hit me. I really had no clue where to start. Should I even be the one to start? Was I just supposed to say, "okay, kid, go work it out?" Or was I supposed to work it out? How much of this was she expected to handle on her own? What WAS my job in all of this? It certainly wasn't the same as it was in WV. I tried hard not to think too much about it. But when I did, I always found myself sliding down a big hole of darkness. I was convinced she was going to wake up in the morning and not need me anymore. After all, she was a city kid now and I was just the mom. I knew I still had to provide food and shelter, and pay for stuff, but beyond that, I was done. Finito. There was no room in her Inn for me. I had been put out to pasture. Checked into the nursing home. Oh, the drama of it all. My life was over and hers was just beginning, and all I could do was watch from the audience and cry.

These feelings went on for months and months and months. Uncertainty. Fear. Anxiety. I also cried A LOT those first two years. I mean, the menopause certainly wasn't helping, but, it still seemed like a lot more breakdowns than any menopausal woman I had ever seen. Looking back, it was probably the most stressful time in my entire adult life. I was trying to keep my emotions in check so the world didn't see the total hot mess of a mom I felt like inside, while trying to raise her to be a responsible adult. Not to mention trying to learn everything I could about this business, so we didn't totally screw this up before we even got started. Folks, my brain was full. Like overflowing with more information than any human could be expected to absorb.

And, if my emotions weren't enough, she was also a tad bit emotional. She was thirteen when we got here - just barely a teenager for heaven's sake. Plus, she was uber-hormonal and had no fear. Which is good and bad when you've just moved ten hours from everything familiar, alone with your crazy single mom and a couple of cats. She thought she could conquer this city with her eyes closed and all I could do was worry about her being kidnapped on the subway.

She wasn't really a kid by NYC standards. She was still a kid, don't get me wrong, but she was a teenager who was perfectly capable of taking the train home alone. She could find her way to the bathroom at break time during rehearsals. She could finish her dinner and be back on stage when break was over without me being there to time her. All I really had to do was sign a simple release that would allow her to leave alone and that was that. Right before my eyes, I was watching her become the self-sufficient adult that I had raised her to be.

It didn't help that I am a natural born crier. Every time she did something, even the tiniest thing, on her own, I would burst into tears. Heck one night I cried during a Huggies commercial. I got out the baby book and all. It was a bona fide meltdown over missing poopy diapers. Who in their right mind misses changing poopy diapers? Apparently in that moment I did. I was a big puddle, right there in the middle of my tiny living room floor. A complete and total hot mess.

I remember one night in particular where my emotions got the better of me. I was already having one of those days where I was feeling rather unneeded. I was home from work before her and it was already dark. I was in my PJ's and every minute she wasn't at home felt like an hour. Mind you, it was like 6:30pm, not midnight. It wasn't like I had been sitting there for hours waiting on her. It was more like minutes.

She came in the door clearly exhausted. She threw her book bag and dance bag to the floor. I could tell by the look on her face, something had happened. On her way home she had found out that she had *yet again* not been cast in her school musical and the look of devastation was one that I had seen several times before since starting high school. Just a few short weeks before she had come home so confident in her audition. More importantly, she was proud that she had navigated the entire audition process on her own.

When she declared that she could "do this on her own," it was like someone knocked the wind out of my sails. We had always prepared for auditions together. I was her practice audience. It took everything I had to keep my mouth shut the day she announced she "had it under control." This step of independence was a normal part of growing up, especially in this business, and I had to just accept it and be supportive, even though on the inside I was crushed. I knew in my heart she had it under control, but the letting go was so darn hard!

She walked in and said, "I didn't get cast and I am going to bed." Okay, kid. You are NOT going to drop a bomb like this and then go to bed. I need to talk through this and analyze it from beginning to end and back again. I'm an out loud processor. I need to talk! For hours and hours and that means you can't just go to bed.

Again? How was this even possible? At that moment I was trying to be a supportive mom, feeling more like a stage mom who wanted to march up to that school and let someone have it. We were in one of the top performing arts schools in NYC. She had not set foot on a stage and she was in the Musical Theater Department. I get it, you can't always get the lead and sometimes you won't get a part. But could she really go through ALL FOUR

YEARS of high school and NEVER get cast? This whole thing was starting to feel like some undercover Russian conspiracy and Mama Bear needed to come out swinging to take out whatever person was responsible for this injustice.

What ensued was one of the only real fights she and I have had in nineteen years. There was screaming, stomping and tears. Had we had a door that actually closed, I am certain there would have been slamming of doors, too. (You might be asking why the doors don't close. Good question. They do. But, all of our doors have those over the door hanging hooks so we can efficiently store coats and such since #babybird took domain over the only closet in the house.) There here might have even been a thrown shoe if my memory is correct. It was UGLY. I mean, UGLY. Words were flying around like the monkeys in *The Wizard of Oz* and neither of us was really listening to the other or worrying about what was coming out of our mouths to each other. I have thanked God many times that we never had to watch this one back on instant replay because there would have been levels of remorse that even the gates of heaven would have trouble holding in based on what came out of our mouths that night.

Let me break it down. I was mad because she didn't get a part. She was mad because she didn't get a part. She was also mad at me for being mad at them for not casting her. She was so full of anger on her own, that my anger just infuriated her even more. It was like a tornado. It started small and kept building and building until SHE finally had the sense to storm into the bathroom to end the battle.

In that moment, I was so lost. I couldn't fix this. She was hurt and disappointed and the best we could do was scream at each other? This is not the mother-daughter relationship we had fostered over the years. And we had never, ever had a fight like this one. I mean, I have had my mom rants. The normal "do the dishes, clean the cat boxes, sweep the floor" and such. but this was more than that. This was a bloodbath and we were both soaked.

Yes, I was angry that she didn't get a part. But what I was really angry about was that I couldn't do anything to fix it. I could stand on the sidelines and be the loudest cheerleader of them all, but that was all I had for her. Instead of just being a safe, soft place to land, I went into Mama Bear mode and, well, you know how that ended. Both of our hearts were in the right place. She just wanted to be on that stage, and I just wanted to help get her there. But screaming at one another wasn't going to solve either of those problems.

That day was a turning point for me. It was the day I had to face the music and find my place. I could no longer live under a rock having absolutely no clue where I fit. It was slowly destroying me. I wholeheartedly believe that every human who walks this earth has a place. Some of us just have to work a little harder than others to find it. She found hers when she was five years old and marched into my kitchen to "sing me a song." And I was still searching.

How could I be well into my forties and still feel like I didn't know my place in this world? From the first moment I laid eyes on her I knew God had prepared me to be her mother. There was no doubt there. But for a few months there, my life began to feel like being in a daily AA meeting. I would look in the mirror and say to myself, "Hello, my name is Steffanie. I am a single mom who has a nearly grown child who doesn't need me anymore and I don't know how to go on living." (Like I said, drama runs deep in this family.)

BOOM. There it was. Somewhere in my warped menopausal mind I had convinced myself I wasn't needed. I know now, there was absolutely zero truth to that statement. But at the time it felt so real. It was as if my success as a parent was suddenly my deepest heartbreak at the same time. I prepared her to be the person she was being, yet I felt left behind. I allowed myself to be consumed by that notion for a long, long time. And that complete blow up between us forced me to look in the mirror like Mary Poppins standing looking at her own reflection. Mary was practically perfect in every way and I was just a lump of a hot mess. I was a scared mom. A mom who was fighting her own feelings of insecurity, while her #babybird was in the bathroom crying her eyes out. I had no choice but to put on my big girl panties and work this out with her.

At that moment, she needed me to push forward when she couldn't, not feed her disappointment with my Mama Bear anger. I had to become ninja mom and make a path for her to get closer and closer to this dream. And that is just what I did. I pulled out my machete of common sense and just started whacking away at the negativity that had taken up residence in both our minds. She hadn't been cast. But I couldn't allow that to define or defeat her. She was not a failure. She was experiencing the hardest part about living this lifestyle. Rejection. It's real. And it sucks. But it could not be the weight that would bring this dream to a crashing halt. It had to be what propelled us forward, and the only person that could help her release that at that moment was me.

She was so grown up for her age and if you didn't know her, you would just assume she had shoulders made of steel that could carry everything. The reality was that she couldn't do that anymore than I could stand on a stage and sing. She needed me to impart upon her the lessons that had taken me years to learn on my own. She needed my knowledge. She needed my adult way of processing information so she could make sound decisions. She needed someone that loved her unconditionally, no matter what.

Wait. She needed ME!

She needed me.

SHE needed me.

SHE NEEDED me.

SHE NEEDED ME!

It was like the theme from *Rocky* was playing in my head and I was getting warmed up to jump into this ring and go nine rounds with this world. And I wasn't about to lose.

What I never realized until that night was that God had been preparing me in a million tiny ways before we ever set foot in NYC. My career shifted to the healthcare business when #babybird was about five. I fell in love with it for a myriad of reasons, but mostly because I love taking care of people. I always have. I find great satisfaction in walking alongside my patients and being a helping hand to them. Who am I kidding? I love to help anyone do just about anything, including packing, moving, party-planning, cleaning, babysitting, and errand running, just to name a few. But this job made me the kind of happy that you feel deep in the core of your soul. Serving others will always lead to a greater blessing than serving yourself. This is one of those traits that I was happy to pass on to her and it has already served her well in her short life. She lives by the motto "love first, ask questions later."

I believe everyone is born with spiritual gifts - the traits that God wove into the fabric of our being that makes us who He needs us to be in this world. I believe that #babybird and I BOTH have the gift of love, but I have a gift I never really understood or wanted until I hit my mid-thirties. The gift of administration. I am a "doer" which means I get stuff done. I make a list and I tick those boxes off one at a time until a task is accomplished. This gift is NOT glamorous. It can also be a ridiculous form of torture at times. There is nothing flashy about being the one to sit behind a computer and organize or plan things. The keeper of the spreadsheet and the master of the budgets.

You know what? This was the EXACT gift that we needed for

this season of life. How could I be so blind and not realize how well God had prepared me? Why was I looking for somewhere to 'fit in' when my place was right in front of my eyes? I could stand behind her and dot all the i's and cross all the t's to set her up to go be the performer she had dreamed of becoming for so long - and enjoy it.

People! There were all kinds of things for me to do! And so many things I am good at! My heart couldn't hardly stand it when things started popping up. I began to lose myself in the planning and organizing. I started making spreadsheet after spreadsheet after spreadsheet. I was the business card collector and the manager of the contacts database. Along with my awesome friend, Steve Cunningham, I manage her website. I created promotional graphics. I managed the calendar. And I was in heaven! Pure bliss would be an understatement.

Sure, at some point she was going to have to do all this stuff on her own, but right now I was here and eager to be part of the adventure. After all, there would be plenty of time to teach her the ins and outs of keeping her affairs in order. For right now, though, I had a place. And it was an important place.

The reality is I will ALWAYS have a place in her life. Heck, I am the reason she even exists! I conceived, incubated, protected, fed, controlled, and provided for her all these years and no one could take that away from me.

I don't want to preach but I am going to step up on my soapbox for a moment or two. If your kid has chosen to chase this dream, realize this. You are needed, wanted AND have a place. It looks differently for everyone, but I can assure you, even if it's only to be there with open arms when things don't go quite how they had hoped, that's enough. We don't have to be all up in the performing side of this to play an extremely important role in our child's journey.

I realize my story is not everyone's story. Yes, I did give up my life. But I was in a position to do that. Had I been married (which, by the way, is STILL the deepest desire of my heart) I couldn't have done any of this. I mean, maybe I could have, but it really would never have occurred to me to have my family live between two cities. Half the family in WV and the other half back and forth to NYC. Serious props to all the families that actually do that (there are a lot of you that we know, love and respect who are doing it!), but I am certain that would have broken me, there is no doubt. I know my limitations and that would have sent me to the crazy house.

Moving may not have been in the cards had my life looked differently, but I will tell you this, I still WOULD have dragged every single person I knew to her shows because I was so proud. I would tell her how inspired I was by her focus, determination, and courage even when she didn't get the part. I would hug her tight when she succeeded and even tighter when she failed. And you know what? That would have been enough. Do what you can and stop worrying about what every other mother or father is doing.

Truthfully, I still have moments of doubt. I sometimes still scratch my head when there isn't anything tangible sitting on my plate to help her with. And, I do have mini-freak-outs every now and then. One of those was when she announced she was taking a "gap year." But, because God is one cool dude, he sent people to talk me off the ledge a time or two until my heart could rest in her decision. Looking back, that might have been the best decision she ever made, because she is THRIVING!

Regardless of what you can or can't do to help your kid, if you are doing anything to encourage their passions, please pat yourself on the back. And this doesn't just go for theater, people! I don't care if it's the debate team, football, dance, or art classes. No matter how small it may seem, the encouragement you are giving your offspring classifies you as AMAZING in my book. You ARE doing something above and beyond the normal "feed, water and protect" guidelines that are set forth in the parenthood manual. You deserve to "feel all the feels" and relish in their achievements.

I am VERY fortunate that my kid and I collaborate very well most of the time. I know for a fact that is not the case with many families where the child has sights of a performing career. Without any influence from me, she often invites me to get involved in her projects at all different levels. Whether it be just to help with the administrative stuff or to offer my opinions on the creative side of things, she has always made a space for me. The good news is that after five years in this city, I finally feel like I know my place - and that is wherever she needs me the most. I realize it may change from project to project and sometimes, my only job will be to tell her it will all work out and that I love her and am immensely proud of her regardless of how her career unfolds.

And you know what? I am FINALLY totally and completely okay with that. I am comfy and cozy right where I am in her life knowing that she will always need me. As the tides of her needs change (and they will - probably often, in fact), I will just sit back and roll with it, relishing in all of her successes along the way, remaining steadfast in her corner ready to jump in whenever SHE decides she needs me.

CHAPTER ELEVEN

Sacrifice

What did I really give up?

This is going to be the shortest chapter in the book. I regret nothing. Let's put that right up front. And, in my mind, I didn't sacrifice a single thing.

Sacrifice is a funny word. Not in the "ha-ha" laughing sense, but in the way that people interpret it and use it in their everyday dialogue. It seems like such a strong word to me. A word that represents something HUGE and often times it's used in the context of losing something to gain something else.

When people started talking about "my sacrifice," I was more than a little confused. I kept hearing the comment, "That mom sacrificed her entire life for that young lady."

If you look it up in the dictionary there are several definitions, but the one that most parallels our journey is the act of giving up something of *value* for the sake of something else regarded as *more valuable.* Okay, that confuses things even further for me. If I did in fact make a "huge sacrifice," what did I give up? Is what I gained more valuable? Did we give up something that wasn't good for something better? Was it just MY sacrifice or did she sacrifice something, too?

Heck, no, we didn't! We had a great life in WV. We had friends, and a church we loved. I had a job that was fulfilling and challenging for me. She was in a school where she had a tight knit group of friends and teachers she truly loved. We had a good life.

The biggest challenge we faced was that she wanted to spend every moment she could on a stage and the opportunities just weren't there for her. There were shows, but at a certain point, she was bored. She wanted a challenge. She wanted to work with people who could help her grow in her craft. I think Charleston is unique in that there are several amazing theater companies that pretty consistently produce shows. But for most people it was a hobby. For #babybird, it was her air. She knew what she wanted, and she wanted to start doing it right away. All the time.

And, in all fairness, she was a completely different kid when she was in a show. Like "Dr. Jekyl and Mr. Hyde" different. It was as if a piece of her was missing when she wasn't working on something creative. I really started to notice it around the time she entered middle school. She wanted to be on a stage like an athlete wanted to be on a football field or a basketball court. If you have a passion that just touches your soul, then you can relate to how she was feeling.

The truth of the matter is sacrifice can mean a hundred different things to a hundred different people. At some point in all of our lives we have made sacrifices; some bigger (and often harder) than others. For example; I have sacrificed my love of the latest trend of the high waisted bikini for the sake of my fellow beach goers. No one needs to see me in a bikini! Sacrifice? Absolutely! Life changing sacrifice? Not hardly.

In all seriousness, from the very moment this all started, I never once felt like it was a sacrifice for me. I chose to have a child. My commitment as a mother was to raise this child and give her every opportunity that was within my means. Haven't you heard parents say, "I just want my child to have the things I didn't. I want more for them." Well, that is exactly what I was doing. Giving her more.

I did give up my life. But I gained a new full, exciting life. *I did give up my job.* But I gained a job that I could have never imagined would be in my plan. (Y'all, I work on 5th Avenue overlooking Central Park! Seriously?!?!?)

But that's the beauty of selfless sacrifice. If you sacrifice yourself for the good of someone else, you will gain ten times more than you could ever have imagined in your own life. I didn't care about me. I was focused on her. She has been given a beautiful gift and she deserved a chance to see where it would lead her in this world.

This book is the result of a sacrifice. I have always loved to write, but if we had stayed in WV, what would I have written about? What story would I have to tell? This journey gave me a story. And our story gave me a chance to do something I have always loved, but never really understood how much until now. I jumped for her but look what fell into my lap as a result.

I think one of the biggest sacrifices we BOTH made was leaving our village. In the very early days following our move, we had lots of contact with people at home. As time passed, that contact isn't quite as strong as those early days. That first year we longed to go home every chance we could. Again, "broker than broke" meant that wasn't really on the top of my priority list for my pennies. For some strange reason, food and electric always won the battle when I threw out airplane tickets or hunger? As year two and three rolled around, going home was still very much on our minds but we didn't seem as controlled by it. But that is exactly what is supposed to happen. As time has passed, we have added another village to our journey. Our old village didn't go anywhere, but they have a new purpose. Our new village is our daily bread. The people we do life with. And every one of them play such an important part in our daily lives.

The sacrifice? We gave up important day to day relationships for a dream. But God is faithful. He honored our dreams and he just expanded our village. I can't imagine my life without my NYC village. Had we never left WV, I would never have met any of these people.

Christmas was really about the only time we could get away. Airplane tickets for two from NYC to WV were crazy expensive so we always drive, sacrificing convenience for practicality. Depending on what time we left, these trips could take anywhere from nine to fourteen hours. If you are a native NY'er then you know the reason for the variance. TRAFFIC! We got creative about when we would leave and the drive itself has become something we look forward to doing together. One of the best parts of these drives were the stowaways. We always had at least one person packed into the economy size car who was headed back to those WV hills and needed a ride. Thankfully none of them needed a ride back because our little car was always stuffed to the gills on the way home, between Christmas presents and our annual Dollar

Tree raids.

Again, driving versus flying may not seem like a big sacrifice to you, but to us, it was huge. Financially, it saved me a bundle of pennies that I needed to put towards something else that we needed. It did kind of stink from a time perspective. An 11- or 12-hour drive versus 4 or 5 hours if we flew was a big loss. The trade off? We either drove or we didn't go. We just accepted that we had to sacrifice a day on each end of our vacation if we wanted to go home and get our tanks filled by our village.

I hear a lot from friends about the size of our apartment. It's small. And, it's true, I gave away, sold, and threw out a LOT of stuff. I know, stuff shouldn't matter, but it did to me on some level. With a past like mine, stuff represented accomplishment. I didn't have a husband. Or a bunch of kids. But I had a house full of furniture. I had a nice car, and I had space. In this world people often measure success by the size of our homes, or the kind of car we drive, or the job we have, or the school our kids attend. It can be somewhat of a competition. My daddy calls that "keeping up with the Joneses." Always going one step further than the neighbors. Then they go one step further than you. And so on and so on.

But the flipside of that sacrifice is far more powerful than I ever expected. I learned very early on that the average NY'er isn't really hung up on stuff. (Keep in mind I said average. YES, there are a couple million people who don't live that way, but there are definitely a couple million more that DO live this way.) We live in much smaller places than the rest of the country, so many NY'ers are minimalists. Less clothes, less shoes, less stuff. My NYC apartment would fit into my WV town house three times over. THREE TIMES OVER!

The sacrifice of space and stuff changed the way we lived for the better. We don't buy excessively like we did when we had all kinds of space to put stuff. My rule since day one has been "if you bring something new into the house, something old has to leave." It's funny to actually share that with you, but it's made a huge difference in how we shop in general, be it for ourselves or for household stuff. It's certainly curbed #babybird's spending habits.

I will never forget the day this rule really sunk in for her. We were just out on one of our little "excursions" popping in and out of cute little stores somewhere on the UWS. We walked into Francesca's, which has always been one of #babybird's favorite places to shop. She found the clearance rack and there were a few sweet deals hanging there taunting her. She tried a few things on and then I laid it out there. "What are you going to give away to make room for these?" At that moment I watched her face go from elated to devastated in 1.5 seconds. I was forcing her to make a choice. A sacrifice if you will. What was going out to make room for those jeans "that she just had to have, because they were such a great deal."

She lowered her head and said, "I don't know, but I guess I don't really need these." She quietly put them back on the rack and we left. She was silent for a few blocks and then she abruptly stopped and said, "Mom! I know, I know." I looked at her with a very puzzled look on my face because at this point, I had already forgotten about the jeans. "Mom, I know which jeans at home I can get rid of to buy those. Can we go back?"

This is one of my proudest moments as a mom. She put thought and care into her decision. She didn't ask me to make an exception "just this one time." She knew the rule. As hard as it was to abide by it, she knew she didn't have a choice.

Sacrifice? Yep. Life changing sacrifice? Not hardly. But I firmly believe that my little "rule" instilled in her a thought process when it comes to buying. Is it a need or a want? Does it have a place or is it going to get stuffed into a closet somewhere only to be found when we did our annual wardrobe change-over? It doesn't matter, honestly. Because her small sacrifice that day was a gift that I pray stays with her when she has her own family someday.

The sacrifice of living smaller in NYC helped me realize the true difference between a want and a need. I NEED so much less than I ever let myself even consider. My WANT list is considerably different, too. I don't NEED a kitchen table and a dining room table. One is enough. And, I certainly don't NEED a dishwasher. I WANT one, but in my apartment, it's just not realistic, so - Dawn it is!

I could go on and on about the trade-offs, but the end result is the same. Our life here is amazing. But that doesn't mean I haven't had moments where the sacrifice creeped up on me and I had to do a gut check. And every time that happens, I think about her. I will always feel like SHE sacrificed FAR MORE than I did. She was a kid when we made the decision to move. She was thirteen and just starting 8th grade. She hadn't been to prom. She hadn't had her first date or her first kiss. She had already missed so much of being a kid because she chose rehearsals over birthday parties. And, while her friends were off playing sports after school, she was taking care of her Nana during the last days of her life.

When her girlfriends were going places with their dads, she was stuck with her mom 24/7.

SHE left everything familiar behind. SHE had to walk into a new school and didn't know a single person. (And, we all know how cruel kids are to the new kid.) SHE had to jump blindly into the performing community and show people what she was made of. At thirteen, these were not things that she was supposed to face. Most of these things were adult things. And for most adults, even one of those challenges would be a lot for them to wade through. The hardest part for me was that I could do nothing to help her. She had to be the one to push forward and make her way.

I knew God would deliver on His promise to never leave us. I knew eventually we would find our community. But she was a kid. She blindly followed my lead. I thank God every day that The Peterson Girl's Titanic voyage didn't end in disaster.

You see, in the end what we learned was WV wasn't more or less valuable than NYC. We are who we are because of these two places. They are equally embedded in our hearts forever. But we did have to leave the day to day living of one behind to fully experience everything this adventure had to offer in the other.

I will never see this move as a sacrifice.

I will always see it as a blessing.

CHAPTER TWELVE

What If?

What if I fail?
My dear, what if you fly?

Along this journey there have been lots of What-If's. I started out calling them worries. I even made a list except instead of pros and cons, I called it my worry list. Worries of all the things that could go terribly wrong if we jumped in and followed the path that God was laying out for us. Afraid of being forgotten by those we loved most back home. Terrified that I might not be able to support us in New York. Fearful of what she would miss of her childhood experiences. What if we didn't make friends? What if we didn't find a church? What if NY'ers didn't like us at all?

Once we got here some of those worries went away, or just got "shelved" in my brain for a bit as I became consumed with other worries. Like, what if I never figure out the subway system? It's my only way to get around. I can't spend the rest of my life being lost. One day I even calculated how much it would cost me to take an Uber to and from work every day. That idea was short lived after I realized what that meant on a monthly basis. I would have to sacrifice food just to quench my fear of getting lost.

I am happy to report that I am pretty masterful at using the subway AND the bus to get myself around now. I even give out directions every now and then. I should, however, apologize to those poor souls that asked me for directions during the first few months we lived here. I was so happy to be recognized as a local that I gave out what I thought were good directions. I am pretty sure someone out there is telling a story at some random holiday dinner about the time they visited NYC and this really nice lady sent them to Coney Island instead of Queens. If that was you, I really am sorry.

My most common worry back then, still rolls around in the back of my mind from time to time. Will #babybird be safe moving around the city alone? Honestly, she is far more directional than I ever was. But she was just a kid when we moved here. Thirteen going on thirty in her own mind. In this way she was a typical teenager. She thought that I was being over protective and nothing was ever going to happen to her. Of course, I prayed for that every time she left the house or left somewhere else to head home. But it truly was fear #1 for me – then and now. At one point, I finally had to take a break from the morning news for a while. I would see stories of kidnappings, assaults and robberies and would freak out and frantically start texting her. When she didn't respond, I went down the dark, dark path of the worst, convincing myself that she was long gone in some unmarked white van. By the time I had gathered an army to go out looking for her, she would be halfway to California.

She humored me pretty much daily. She would always text very sweetly that she was okay. In her mind I am certain she was asking God to calm her crazy mother down! When she forgot, which surprisingly wasn't often, she would apologize and tell me how much she loved me. She knew I needed that little nugget of comfort before I could set my mind to my days' work.

I was also "that mom" that refused to let her not have a 1st period at school. She did not need to get accustomed to sleeping in until 8am. After all, in just a few short years she was going to be out of school and in the real world where you can't sleep in every day. I, on the other hand, didn't start work until 9am. With just one small bathroom it was in everyone's best interest if only one of us needed to shower and get ready at the same time, especially since one of us was dressing "to the 9's" for Humanities class. She knew I was a worrier, so when she departed before I did, she always yelled from the door as she was leaving, "Bye Mama, I love you." At that moment my unease began, and it wouldn't subside until I got the @school text. Then, and only then, could I relax. This worry still exists and I am pretty sure it will continue, but after nearly five years I am trying to harness it a bit; at least most days. I don't know if it's just become a habit, or if she just wants to keep me calm, but to this day I still get the "I made it" texts pretty much every day.

I could make a list of all my worries that would likely be longer than Santa's delivery list, but that would not change a single one of them. Nothing I could do would make them go away. Some days I was downright scared to get out of bed when we first moved here. I mean, there were times that stepping outside the door was a win on so many levels.

But one day I realized how bad worries really are for you. It's a scientific fact that worrying can actually make you physically sick. Yes, physically sick. Worries were things I honestly thought I had no control over. Worry consumed me; it paralyzed me some days. It clouded my communication with God and my ability to hear Him, which is my lifeline most days. It stopped me from accepting help, prayer and love from those standing behind us, cheering us on.

I had to find a way to stop the worry from overtaking me. But how in the world was I going to do that? Well, I wasn't. God was. You see, before we went to Orlando, I found this saying on Facebook:

"What if I fail? Oh, my dear, what if you fly?"

I even made a little sign for #babybird with this on it and gave it to her the first day we were in Orlando as encouragement. Funny part is, she wasn't the one who needed encouragement. I was. At some point between Orlando and making the announcement to move, as I became completely overwhelmed with worry, I remembered this sign and slowly began to try to change the way I processed the unknown. I was determined to turn down the noise of the worries and turn up the music of the possibilities. I still sometimes hear that noise, but I am happy to report that I hear beautiful music much more often now.

What-If's are not much different, really. Well, actually they are VERY different. Worry stops at the negative. You throw it out there and sit on it. Fester on it. Let it consume you like a raging fire. For a lot of people worry puts them UNDER THE PROVERBIAL

BUS if you will. They are crippled to move past the negative.

A What-If offers the same thing, but it offers a solution; a positive. What-If we DON'T have an answer? What If we DO?! Oddly enough sometimes the What-If-We-Do was as scary (maybe even a little scarier) than the What-If-We-Don't!

What if I don't find a job?
WHAT IF I DO?

What if it doesn't pay enough to live on my own with a child in a big city?
WHAT IF WE FIND FINANCIAL SECURITY LIKE I HAVE NEVER KNOWN?

What if Hannah doesn't fit in here?
WHAT IF SHE FINALLY FINDS THE PLACE IN THIS WORLD WHERE SHE DOES FIT?

What if we don't find a church?
WHAT IF WE DO FIND A CHURCH WHERE WE CAN LIVE, LOVE AND SERVE AS GOD HAD PLANNED FOR US?

What if we don't make friends and find community?
WHAT IF WE FIND FRIENDS THAT WILL LEAD US THAT MUCH CLOSER TO OUR DREAMS?

What if we fail?
WHAT IF WE SUCCEED?

You see, for every What-If driven by fear, there is an equal What-If of endless beginnings.

Let me be clear with y'all for a moment. I am not Positive Polly. In fact, if you know me at all, then you know I am a quick spiraler. I can go from the tip top of the mountain of God's grace to pit of hell, fire and brimstone, with one small breeze of trouble. It has been a battle my whole life. Call it emotions. Call me the President of Crazy Town. Call me the ultimate swinging pendulum. All of those probably apply at some point in my life (heck, sometimes I am all three in ONE DAY)!

When I start to worry (spiral to the deep depths of self-pity and fear, I mean) in the What If's, I have to make a conscious choice to stop and turn my mind to the "We do's" for a moment. Then I pull up my big girl panties and rest in God's grace until I regain my balance and crawl back out of the worry into the reality of possibility.

We DID move from WV to NYC. Just two girls, three cats, and a rental truck.

I DID get a job. A really good job that served me well in our first year here. And now I have another one! (That I truly love, by the way!)

Hannah DID get into a very prestigious performing arts high school that gave her lots of training that she will need to succeed in this business.

Hannah DID sign with an agent. A wonderful team of people who believe in her and are walking alongside us on this journey!

We DID find an apartment in a safe neighborhood. And a second one.

If you hear nothing else about our story hear this:
We DID.
I DID.
She DID.
GOD DID.

He promises me (and you) over and over and over in scripture that He will never leave us. That His plans are perfect. That His grace is enough. I am here to report, just in case you were wondering, His Grace IS enough. His plans ARE perfect. And, He IS always right on time. More importantly, He won't leave you. Ever. I stake our entire journey on His goodness, His love, His mercy and His guidance. Steffanie and Hannah Jane Peterson are simply following the path He continues to clear for us. I promise you, there was no magical star alignment that made this move and this journey so far a possibility for two girls from small town WV. There was faith. There was trust. There was determination. There was obedience. All the things that God pours out on each one of us moment after moment after moment of our lives.

I believe that #babybird has been given a beautiful gift. I believe in the depth of my soul that God's path for her is to move others emotionally through her music. But I know ONE THING for certain. There are a ton of kids like her. Talented, I mean really talented, kids all across this world. I believe what got us here was our unwavering faith in God's plan. Our courage to follow Him first and the world second. Our unending supply of love for people. ALL people.

When I recount the many prayers that went unanswered (probably most glaring was my daily prayer for a Godly husband to join our little team) to make this move even a possibility in our lives, I am astounded at God's judgement. He knew what needed to happen and what needed to NOT happen. His timing was perfect. Even when I was in the fetal position clutching my Bible begging him for things that I thought I should have because everyone else around me had them.

God moved mountains where I could not. He broke down doors that I didn't have the keys to open on my own. He gave me the right words when I was speaking to industry executives about things I didn't completely understand. He interceded on my behalf.

I realize I am a biased, overly proud mama who wants to see her #babybird fly to the tip tops of every tree she sets her sights on. But I also know that won't come without hard work, a humble heart and a spirit of love for all people.

I didn't write this book as a spiritual testimony, which is why I saved this chapter for last. What I wrote was our story. Factual. Emotional. Adventurous. Every word is true. But I could never have told this story and NOT included our faith and our belief in Jesus Christ. He is the center of this little family. Today and Always.

If our story makes you feel invigorated to chase your own dreams, please remember this: We did not do this alone. Not for one minute were we ever walking the journey without our village and God in every decision, every performance, every meeting, every encounter.

So, was it all worth it? Absolutely! And the best part is, I can say that without one ounce of hesitation.

To Him be the glory for The Peterson Girls Adventures.

CHAPTER THIRTEEN

What's Next?

The story has just begun . . .

This is not the end of our adventure. Each day there is a new beautiful beginning right in front of us. Every day we get a blank page. A new day to make memories, take adventures, love people, and make our little corner of this world a better place.

I could write for days about the emotions I had when #babybird graduated high school. I am certain every mother and father who has sat in an auditorium and watched their child cross that stage, symbolically leaving their childhood behind and stepping into this world as more of an adult than a child, can attest. It literally happens in an instant. And once they cross over, there is no going back. We don't get a "do-over" in an attempt to do better the second time around. They are headed into the real world, and we have to hope and pray that we gave them everything they need to succeed.

I was riding the subway home from work about a month before her graduation. As I started to make my list of things to do for her party, I had a moment. (Gosh, I had SO MANY moments her senior year. Whew, I was not ready for any of them, either.) My heart began to race, and I started to think about all the things I wanted to tell her about life. Things I know I have told her before in some manner, but in that moment, I was suddenly in a panic. I felt like I needed to impart a lifetime of wisdom on her and I had suddenly run out of time. In thirty days she would be a high school graduate for Pete's sake and I had stuff to say.

I wrote the following poem (At least I think it's a poem. Another thing I never thought I would do – write a poem.) on the remainder of my train ride home. I planned to tuck this into the professional camera bag I was giving her as her graduation gift. The words just keep coming and then the tears started, and my mind was racing so fast my fingers could hardly keep up with my thoughts. (I gave some people on that rush hour train some good people watching time as I had my mini meltdown.) This truly sums up everything I have always wanted her to know. You could easily take her out of the equation and share this with anyone in your life that is leaping towards something that seems out of their reach. Or a dream that seems too big to actually come true.

As a matter of fact, steal this. Share it with someone who needs to be encouraged to do something big in their life. Print it, mail it, email it. Do whatever you have to do to get this in someone's hands that needs to hear that it's ok to dream. It's ok to take a chance. And, it's ok if it doesn't work out exactly as you planned. Honestly, the most cherished moments for us so far lie in the times when we were reaching. Don't get me wrong, when she steps on a stage, I get chills and have a moment where I say to myself – it was all worth it. But it could end today, and it would STILL be all worth it.

We are all on the same trajectory from the cradle to the grave. It's what we do in between that matters. God designed us for more. ALL of us.

GO! GO! GO!

Encourage.

Inspire.

Dream.

My dearest Hannah Jane,

Inside this bag is a million pictures you have yet to take. A million memories you have yet to make.

Countless obstacles that will knock you down. When they do (and they will; it's just part of living) Get back up. Every single time. Get. Back. Up. Remember, each time you get up, it will be harder to knock you back down. (YES, I might have stolen that from a country song from the 90s. Oh well.)

Never let this world tell you that you can't, because you CAN. And you will. I am confident of that. You have moved at the speed of light since the day you were born. Let that determination drive you forward. Don't look back. You can't change the past. But you can learn from it. Everything that is behind you had a purpose. It shaped you. But dwelling where you faltered will keep you from being who you were born to be.

Say yes. Every chance you can, say YES! Sometimes it will pay off. Other times it might not. But if you don't say yes, you will never know. Remember your glass is always half full, not half empty.

You have the only co-pilot you will ever need. God will NEVER leave you. He may remain silent at times when he is refining you, but rest assured he is only a whisper of his name away. Trust in His word. Trust in His promises. They are the only two things in this world that you can ALWAYS depend on. People will fail you. Forgive them; life is too short to hold on to hurt. God will never fail you. Put all your eggs in His basket. He's got you.

Use your gifts. God doesn't give gifts to sit idle on a shelf. You move people with your music. In a difficult world, your music will heal. When life is rotten (and it will be, I promise you that) let your love of music wash over you. Let it engulf you. Let it heal you and those around you.

You have made me mad. You have made me cry. You have made me laugh hysterically for hours on end. Most important of all...you have made me proud. Of your courage; your determination; your drive; your vision; and your passion.

The way you love people first and ask questions later is beautiful. Never stop doing that; ALWAYS lead with love. Keep your love for people at the forefront of your journey. That love will build bridges, mend hearts and make this world a better place. The woman you are becoming is a world-changer and this world NEEDS you.

Experience everything this life has to offer. Don't be afraid of going on new adventures. Living adventurously is in your blood; embrace it. (Hence a 12 hour move with your crazy single mom and three cats.)

I know it wasn't always easy; but we are survivors; and we are not just surviving - WE ARE THRIVING! When it's time to slide into your grave, go in with all the bumps, bruises and scratches that a life well lived will leave upon you.

Put your camera in this bag.
Take a million pictures.
Make a million memories.
The future is yours.

I love you, Linda. Forever. (Inside joke, sorry!)

Remember, it's not the end.
It's just another beautiful beginning.

About the Author

Join us on the journey!

Steffanie Peterson is a single mom who made the courageous decision to move her 13-year-old daughter to NYC to chase her dreams of being on Broadway. A native of Charleston, WV, she knew Hannah Jane wasn't going to get there living in their cozy hometown.

When she's not looking after her daughter, you can find Steffanie managing a busy plastic surgery practice on Fifth Avenue in Manhattan, volunteering at her church, and now, sharing the ups and downs of the grand adventure they have been on the past five years.

The journey has just begun and Steffanie and Hannah Jane would love for you to come along! Find their social media links at Steffanie's blog:

www.thepetersongirlsadventures.com
#thepetersongirlsadventures

35th Star Publishing
www.35thstar.com

Made in the USA
Middletown, DE
02 March 2020